Time is Money

Ezekiel Iziogo

Time is Money

The Entrepreneur's Guide to Freeing Up Time

TABLE OF CONTENTS

Introduction   5
Chapter 1: Understanding the Value of Time   5
Chapter 2: Setting Clear Goals and Priorities   5
Chapter 3: Planning and Scheduling   5
Chapter 4: Leveraging Technology for Efficiency   6
Chapter 5: Delegating and Outsourcing   6
Chapter 6: Minimizing Distractions and Staying Focused   6
Chapter 7: Developing Productive Habits   6
Chapter 8: Work-Life Balance   6
Chapter 9: Continuous Improvement   7
Conclusion   7
Appendices   7
References   7

Introduction

Purpose of the Book

In today's fast-paced world, time is one of the most valuable resources at our disposal. For entrepreneurs, managing time effectively is crucial to success. "Time is Money: The Entrepreneur's Guide to Freeing Up Time" is written to address this essential aspect of entrepreneurship. This book aims to provide practical strategies and insights to help entrepreneurs reclaim their time, enhance productivity, and achieve a balanced life.

The motivation behind writing this book stems from the common challenges entrepreneurs face. Many struggle with juggling numerous responsibilities, leading to burnout and inefficiency. By sharing proven techniques and best practices, this book aims to equip entrepreneurs with the tools they need to manage their time wisely. This, in turn, will enable them to focus on what truly matters – growing their business and enjoying a fulfilling life.

Entrepreneurs often wear multiple hats – from managing day-to-day operations to strategic planning and everything in between. The sheer volume of tasks can be overwhelming, and without effective time management, it's easy to get lost in the chaos. This book is a comprehensive guide to mastering the art of time management. It provides actionable advice on setting goals, planning, delegating, minimizing distractions, and much more.

By reading this book, entrepreneurs will learn how to:

- Identify and prioritize tasks that drive business success.
- Delegate and outsource tasks effectively to focus on high-impact activities.
- Use technology to automate repetitive tasks and enhance efficiency.
- Create a productive work environment that minimizes distractions.
- Develop habits and routines that promote productivity.
- Maintain a healthy work-life balance to sustain long-term success.

Who This Book is For

This book is designed for a diverse audience, including:

- **New Entrepreneurs**: Those who are just starting their entrepreneurial journey and need guidance on how to manage their time effectively from the outset.
- **Small Business Owners**: Individuals running small businesses who want to improve their time management skills to boost productivity and achieve better results.
- **Aspiring Entrepreneurs**: People considering starting their own business and seeking to

understand the importance of time management in achieving their goals.
- **Freelancers and Solopreneurs**: Individuals working independently who need to juggle multiple tasks and responsibilities without the support of a larger team.
- **Managers and Team Leaders**: Professionals who lead teams and want to learn how to manage their own time and the time of their team members more effectively.
- **Anyone Interested in Improving Time Management Skills**: Whether you're an entrepreneur or not, this book offers valuable insights and strategies for anyone looking to make better use of their time.

The principles and techniques discussed in this book are applicable across various industries and business sizes. Whether you are running a tech startup, a retail store, a consulting firm, or a creative agency, effective time management is key to success. By mastering these skills, you can enhance your productivity, reduce stress, and create a more balanced and fulfilling professional and personal life.

How to Use This Book

"Time is Money: The Entrepreneur's Guide to Freeing Up Time" is structured to provide a comprehensive yet practical approach to time management. Each chapter focuses on a specific aspect of time management, offering detailed insights and actionable advice. Here's how to navigate through the book and make the most of its content:

1. **Start with the Basics**: If you're new to time management, begin with Chapter 1 to understand the fundamental concepts and the value of time. This will provide a solid foundation for the strategies discussed in the later chapters.

2. **Follow the Sequence**: While each chapter can stand alone, the book is designed to be read sequentially. Each chapter builds on the previous one, providing a logical progression from understanding time management to implementing advanced techniques.

3. **Take Notes and Reflect**: As you read through the chapters, take notes and reflect on how the concepts apply to your own business and personal life. Identify specific areas where you can improve and set goals for implementing the strategies discussed.

4. **Implement the Strategies**: The real value of this book lies in applying the strategies to your daily routine. Each chapter includes practical tips and exercises to help you implement the concepts. Make a commitment to try out the techniques and

adjust them to fit your unique circumstances.

5. **Use the Templates and Worksheets**: The appendices include templates and worksheets designed to help you plan and organize your time effectively. Use these tools to create schedules, set goals, track progress, and evaluate your time management practices.

6. **Revisit and Review**: Time management is a continuous process of improvement. Revisit the chapters periodically to refresh your knowledge and assess your progress. As your business grows and evolves, you may find new insights and techniques that are relevant to your changing needs.

7. **Engage with the Community**: Join online forums, discussion groups, or local networking events to connect with other entrepreneurs who are also focused on improving their time management skills. Sharing experiences and learning from others can provide valuable support and motivation.

Overview of the Chapters

To give you a sense of what to expect, here is a brief overview of the chapters:

- **Chapter 1: Understanding the Value of Time**: Discusses the importance of time management and the impact of wasting time on business success. Highlights how successful entrepreneurs value and manage their time.

- **Chapter 2: Setting Clear Goals and Priorities**: Guides you through defining your vision and mission, setting SMART goals, and prioritizing tasks effectively.

- **Chapter 3: Planning and Scheduling**: Covers techniques for creating daily schedules, using time blocks, and planning for unexpected events to ensure flexibility and productivity.

- **Chapter 4: Leveraging Technology for Efficiency**: Explores tools and apps that can help with time management, automating repetitive tasks, and enhancing communication and collaboration.

- **Chapter 5: Delegating and Outsourcing**: Provides strategies for identifying tasks to delegate, finding the right people, and managing outsourced work to ensure quality and efficiency.

- **Chapter 6: Minimizing Distractions and Staying Focused**: Identifies common distractions and offers strategies to stay focused and create a productive work environment.

- **Chapter 7: Developing Productive Habits**: Discusses the importance of building a routine, maintaining consistency, and avoiding procrastination to enhance productivity.

- **Chapter 8: Work-Life Balance**: Emphasizes the importance of balancing work and personal life, setting boundaries, and managing stress to sustain long-term success.

- **Chapter 9: Continuous Improvement**: Focuses on evaluating your time management practices, learning from mistakes, and adapting to changes to continually improve.

- **Conclusion**: Summarizes the key points from the book and provides encouragement for the journey ahead.

- **Appendices**: Includes recommended tools and resources, templates and worksheets, and further reading materials to support your time management efforts.

- **References**: Lists all the references and sources used in the book for further reading and validation of information.

By following the guidance in this book, you can transform your approach to time management and unlock the full potential of your entrepreneurial journey. Whether you're just starting out or looking to refine your existing practices, "Time is Money: The Entrepreneur's Guide to Freeing Up Time" will serve as a valuable resource to help you achieve your goals and enjoy a more balanced, productive, and fulfilling life.

Chapter 1: Understanding the Value of Time

The Importance of Time Management

For entrepreneurs, effective time management is not just a desirable skill—it is a crucial determinant of business success. The ability to manage time well can mean the difference between a thriving, scalable enterprise and one that struggles to stay afloat. Here's why managing time is so vital:

Maximizing Productivity

Effective time management helps entrepreneurs maximize their productivity by ensuring that they spend their time on high-value tasks that drive their business forward. By prioritizing essential activities and eliminating or delegating less critical ones, entrepreneurs can focus their energy on the areas that will have the most significant impact. This not only boosts productivity but also enhances the overall efficiency of the business.

Enhancing Decision-Making

Good time management allows entrepreneurs to allocate sufficient time to make informed decisions. Rushed decisions, often a result of poor time management, can lead to costly mistakes. By managing their time well, entrepreneurs can take the necessary time to gather relevant information, consider various options, and make decisions that are in the best interest of their business.

Reducing Stress and Avoiding Burnout

Entrepreneurship is inherently stressful, with its high demands and constant pressure to perform. Effective time management helps reduce stress by creating a structured approach to handling tasks and responsibilities. This structured approach allows entrepreneurs to maintain a healthier work-life balance, reducing the risk of burnout and ensuring sustained long-term performance.

Meeting Deadlines and Achieving Goals

Setting and meeting deadlines is critical in the business world. Missed deadlines can damage a company's reputation, strain relationships with clients and partners, and result in financial losses. Good time management practices ensure that entrepreneurs can meet their deadlines consistently, which is essential for achieving short-term objectives and long-term goals.

Improving Customer Satisfaction

For businesses, customer satisfaction is paramount. Effective time management ensures that entrepreneurs can respond to customer inquiries promptly, deliver products and services on time, and address any issues that may arise quickly. This responsiveness builds customer trust and loyalty, which are crucial for the business's growth and sustainability.

Gaining a Competitive Edge

In a competitive market, businesses that can operate more efficiently and respond faster to market changes gain a significant advantage over their competitors. Effective time management enables entrepreneurs to be more agile, quickly adapting to new opportunities and challenges. This agility is a critical factor in maintaining a competitive edge in any industry.

The Cost of Wasting Time

While the benefits of effective time management are clear, the consequences of poor time management can be detrimental to an entrepreneur's business. Here's how wasting time can lead to financial losses and missed opportunities:

Financial Losses

Time is money, and wasting time can directly translate into financial losses. Here are some ways in which poor time management can impact the bottom line:

- **Lost Revenue Opportunities**: When entrepreneurs spend too much time on low-priority tasks, they miss out on opportunities to generate revenue. For instance, spending excessive time on administrative work instead of focusing on sales and marketing activities can lead to missed sales opportunities.

- **Increased Operational Costs**: Inefficient use of time can lead to higher operational costs. For example, if a project takes longer than anticipated due to poor time management, the business may incur additional labor costs, resource expenses, and other related costs.

- **Unproductive Workforce**: Poor time management can lead to an unproductive workforce. When employees are not guided effectively, they may spend time on tasks that do not contribute to the business's goals, resulting in wasted payroll expenses.

- **Delayed Payments and Penalties**: Missing deadlines for client deliverables or project milestones can lead to delayed payments and, in some cases, financial penalties. This not only impacts cash flow but can also strain relationships with clients.

Missed Opportunities

In addition to direct financial losses, poor time management can result in missed opportunities that could have otherwise propelled the business forward:

- **Market Opportunities**: In the fast-paced business world, opportunities often arise quickly and require prompt action. Entrepreneurs who are bogged down by poor time management may fail to capitalize on these opportunities, allowing competitors to gain an advantage.

- **Partnerships and Collaborations**: Building strategic partnerships and collaborations often requires timely communication and follow-up. Poor time management can lead to missed meetings, delayed responses, and lost opportunities for valuable partnerships.

- **Innovation and Development**: Time is a critical factor in innovation. Entrepreneurs who are constantly firefighting due to poor time management may lack the time to invest in research and development, leading to missed opportunities for innovation and growth.

Damaged Reputation

An entrepreneur's reputation is built on reliability and trustworthiness. Poor time management can damage this reputation in several ways:

- **Missed Deadlines**: Consistently missing deadlines can make clients and partners view the business as unreliable, leading to a loss of trust and potential future business.

- **Poor Customer Service**: Slow response times and delayed service delivery can result in dissatisfied customers, negative reviews, and a tarnished reputation.

- **Unprofessionalism**: Poor time management can lead to a lack of preparation for meetings and presentations, appearing unprofessional and undermining the entrepreneur's credibility.

How Successful Entrepreneurs Value Time

Successful entrepreneurs understand the intrinsic value of time and treat it as their most precious resource. They adopt specific practices and mindsets to manage their time effectively and ensure they focus on high-impact activities. Here are some insights and examples of how successful entrepreneurs prioritize and value their time:

Prioritization

Successful entrepreneurs prioritize their tasks based on their goals and the potential impact of each activity. They focus on what is most important and delegate or eliminate tasks that do not contribute significantly to their objectives. This approach ensures that their time is spent on activities that drive business success.

- **Example: Warren Buffett**: Warren Buffett, one of the most successful investors in the world, is known for his ability to prioritize effectively. He focuses on a few key investments that he believes have the highest potential for long-term growth, rather than spreading his time and resources across numerous opportunities.

Delegation

Delegation is a critical skill for successful entrepreneurs. By delegating tasks that can be handled by others, entrepreneurs free up their time to focus on strategic decisions and high-value activities.

- **Example: Richard Branson**: Richard Branson, the founder of the Virgin Group, emphasizes the importance of delegation. He hires talented individuals to manage various aspects of his businesses, allowing him to concentrate on vision and strategy.

Time Blocking

Time blocking is a technique used by many successful entrepreneurs to structure their day and ensure they allocate time for critical tasks. By dividing the day into specific blocks of time dedicated to particular activities, they can maintain focus and productivity.

- **Example: Elon Musk**: Elon Musk, the CEO of Tesla and SpaceX, is known for his rigorous time-blocking approach. He schedules his day in five-minute blocks, allowing him to manage multiple high-profile companies efficiently.

Continuous Learning

Successful entrepreneurs invest time in continuous learning and self-improvement. They understand that staying ahead of industry trends and developing new skills is essential for maintaining a competitive edge.

- **Example: Bill Gates**: Bill Gates, co-founder of Microsoft, is an avid reader and lifelong learner. He dedicates time each day to reading and learning about various subjects, from technology to philanthropy.

Work-Life Balance

Maintaining a healthy work-life balance is crucial for long-term success. Successful entrepreneurs recognize the importance of taking care of their physical and mental well-being to sustain their productivity and creativity.

- **Example: Arianna Huffington**: Arianna Huffington, founder of The Huffington Post and Thrive Global, advocates for the importance of sleep and well-being. She emphasizes that taking care of oneself is essential for maintaining high performance and avoiding burnout.

Case Study: Successful Time Management in Practice

To illustrate the principles of effective time management, let's take a closer look at a real-world example of an entrepreneur who has mastered this skill:

Case Study: Elon Musk

Elon Musk is a prime example of an entrepreneur who manages his time exceptionally well. As the CEO of Tesla and SpaceX, Musk oversees two of the most innovative companies in the world, while also being involved in other ventures like Neuralink and The Boring Company. Here's how he manages his time:

- **Time Blocking**: Musk divides his day into five-minute blocks, meticulously planning his schedule to ensure he can address the needs of his various enterprises. This level of detail allows him to maximize productivity and minimize wasted time.

- **Prioritization**: Musk focuses on high-impact tasks that require his unique expertise and vision. He delegates other responsibilities to capable team members, ensuring that his time is spent on activities that drive the most value for his companies.

- **Delegation**: Musk hires highly skilled and trusted individuals to lead different divisions of his companies. By delegating operational tasks to these leaders, he can focus on strategic decisions and innovation.

- **Continuous Learning**: Despite his busy schedule, Musk makes time for learning and staying updated on technological advancements and industry trends. This continuous learning helps him drive innovation within his companies.

- **Work-Life Balance**: While Musk is known for his intense work ethic, he also acknowledges the importance of personal time. He makes efforts to spend time with his family and engage in activities that help him recharge.

Elon Musk's approach to time management demonstrates that with the right strategies and mindset, it is possible to manage multiple high-demand roles effectively. His success underscores the importance of prioritization, delegation, and continuous learning in achieving business goals.

Conclusion

Understanding the value of time and mastering the art of time management are essential skills for entrepreneurs. Effective time management enables entrepreneurs to maximize productivity, enhance decision-making, reduce stress, and maintain a competitive edge. Conversely, poor time management can lead to financial losses, missed opportunities, and a damaged reputation.

By prioritizing high-value tasks, delegating responsibilities, using techniques like time blocking, and investing in continuous learning, successful entrepreneurs can make the most of their time and achieve

their business objectives. As you embark on your entrepreneurial journey, remember that time is your most valuable resource. Use it wisely, and it will pay dividends in the form of business success and personal fulfillment.

Chapter 2: Setting Clear Goals and Priorities

Defining Your Vision and Mission

Setting clear goals and priorities begins with having a well-defined vision and mission. These statements serve as the foundation for all your business activities and decisions, providing direction and purpose. A clear vision and mission align your goals and ensure that every action you take moves you closer to your ultimate objectives.

Vision Statement

A vision statement describes the future state you aspire to achieve with your business. It should be inspiring, clear, and focused on the long-term. Your vision statement serves as a guide for where you want your business to go and helps keep you motivated during challenging times.

Creating a Vision Statement:

1. Think Long-Term: Consider where you want your business to be in 5, 10, or even 20 years.
2. Be Inspiring: Craft a statement that motivates you and your team.
3. Stay Focused: Ensure your vision is specific enough to provide clear direction.

Example:

- Tesla's Vision: "To create the most compelling car company of the 21st century by driving the world's transition to electric vehicles."

Mission Statement

A mission statement defines the purpose of your business. It explains why your business exists, what it does, and who it serves. A good mission statement is concise, clear, and focused on the present and immediate future.

Creating a Mission Statement:

1. Identify Your Purpose: Understand why your business exists and what you aim to achieve.
2. Define Your Audience: Specify who your business serves.
3. Highlight What You Do: Clearly state the products or services you offer.

Example:

- Google's Mission: "To organize the world's information and make it universally accessible and useful."

Aligning Vision and Mission with Goals

Your vision and mission statements should serve as a compass for setting your business goals. Every goal you set should move you closer to realizing your vision and fulfilling your mission. This alignment ensures consistency and purpose in your actions.

Steps to Align Goals:

1. Review Your Vision and Mission: Regularly revisit these statements to ensure they remain relevant.
2. Set Aligned Goals: Ensure that every goal contributes to achieving your vision and mission.
3. Communicate Clearly: Make sure your team understands how their individual goals and tasks align with the broader vision and mission.

Setting SMART Goals

Effective goal setting is critical for business success. SMART goals provide a framework for setting clear, actionable, and achievable objectives. SMART stands for Specific, Measurable, Achievable, Relevant, and Time-bound.

Specific

A specific goal clearly defines what you want to achieve. It answers the questions: who, what, where, when, and why. Specific goals leave no room for ambiguity and provide a clear path to follow.

Example:

- Non-Specific Goal: "Increase sales."
- Specific Goal: "Increase online sales of our flagship product by 20% within the next six months by optimizing our e-commerce platform and launching targeted marketing campaigns."

Measurable

A measurable goal includes criteria for tracking progress and determining when the goal is achieved. It answers the question: how will you measure success?

Example:

- Non-Measurable Goal: "Improve customer satisfaction."
- Measurable Goal: "Increase customer satisfaction scores by 15% within the next quarter by implementing a new customer feedback system and training staff on customer service best practices."

Achievable

An achievable goal is realistic and attainable, considering the resources and constraints you have. It answers the question: is this goal within reach?

Example:

- Unachievable Goal: "Double our revenue in one month."
- Achievable Goal: "Increase our monthly revenue by 10% over the next three months by expanding our product line and enhancing our marketing efforts."

Relevant

A relevant goal aligns with your vision, mission, and broader business objectives. It answers the question: does this goal matter to the business?

Example:

- Irrelevant Goal: "Launch a new social media platform for an accounting firm."
- Relevant Goal: "Enhance our online presence by increasing social media engagement by 25% over the next six months to attract more clients."

Time-bound

A time-bound goal includes a deadline or timeframe for achieving it. It answers the question: when will this goal be achieved?

Example:

- Non-Time-bound Goal: "Expand our market reach."
- Time-bound Goal: "Enter three new regional markets within the next year by establishing local partnerships and adapting our marketing strategy."

Combining SMART Criteria

Combining all the SMART criteria helps in setting comprehensive and actionable goals. Here's an example of a SMART goal:

Example: "Increase our email newsletter subscriber base by 30% within the next six months by implementing a referral program and enhancing our lead capture forms on our website."

Prioritizing Tasks Effectively

Once you have set clear goals, the next step is to prioritize your tasks to ensure you are focusing on what truly matters. Prioritization involves evaluating tasks based on their urgency and importance, and then allocating your time and resources accordingly.

The Eisenhower Matrix

The Eisenhower Matrix, also known as the Urgent-Important Matrix, is a popular tool for prioritizing tasks. It helps you categorize tasks into four quadrants based on their urgency and importance:

1. **Quadrant I: Urgent and Important**

   - Tasks that require immediate attention and are critical to achieving your goals.
   - Example: Addressing a critical customer issue or meeting a crucial project deadline.

2. **Quadrant II: Not Urgent but Important**

   - Tasks that are important for long-term success but do not require immediate attention.
   - Example: Strategic planning, skill development, and relationship building.

3. **Quadrant III: Urgent but Not Important**

   - Tasks that require immediate attention but do not significantly contribute to your goals.
   - Example: Interruptions, minor requests, and some meetings.

4. **Quadrant IV: Not Urgent and Not Important**

   - Tasks that do not contribute to your goals and do not require immediate attention.
   - Example: Time-wasting activities, excessive social media use, and trivial **tasks.**

Using the Eisenhower Matrix:

1. List Your Tasks: Write down all the tasks you need to accomplish.

2. Categorize: Place each task in the appropriate quadrant.
3. Prioritize: Focus on Quadrant I tasks first, then Quadrant II. Minimize or delegate Quadrant III tasks, and eliminate or reduce Quadrant IV tasks.

The ABCDE Method

The ABCDE method is another effective prioritization technique that categorizes tasks by their level of importance and urgency:

1. **A, Tasks:** Must-do tasks that are critical to achieving your goals. These tasks have serious consequences if not completed.
2. **B Tasks:** Should-do tasks that are important but not as critical as A tasks. These tasks have mild consequences if not completed.
3. **C Tasks:** Nice-to-do tasks that have no significant consequences if not completed. These tasks do not contribute directly to your **goals.**
4. **D Tasks:** Delegate tasks that can be handled by someone else. Delegating frees up your time for higher-priority tasks.
5. **E Tasks:** Eliminate tasks that are not necessary and do not contribute to your goals. Removing these tasks increases efficiency.

Using the ABCDE Method:

1. List Your Tasks: Write down all the tasks you need to accomplish.

2. Categorize: Assign each task a letter from A to E based on its importance and urgency.
3. Prioritize: Focus on A tasks first, then move on to B tasks, and so on. Delegate D tasks and eliminate E tasks.

The Ivy Lee Method

The Ivy Lee Method is a simple yet powerful technique for prioritizing tasks and enhancing productivity. It involves selecting the most important tasks to accomplish each day and focusing on them one at a time.

Using the Ivy Lee Method:

1. List Your Tasks: At the end of each workday, write down the six most important tasks you need to accomplish the next day.
2. Prioritize: Order these six tasks by their level of importance.
3. Focus: Start with the first task and work on it until it is completed before moving on to the next task.
4. Review: At the end of the day, review what you have accomplished. Carry over any unfinished tasks to the next day's list.

Real-World Examples of Goal Setting and Prioritization

To understand how these techniques are applied in real-world scenarios, let's look at some examples of successful entrepreneurs who have mastered goal setting and prioritization:

Example: Jeff Bezos and Amazon

Jeff Bezos, the founder of Amazon, is known for his long-term vision and meticulous prioritization. When Bezos started Amazon, his vision was to create the "Earth's biggest bookstore." This clear vision guided his goal setting and decision-making process.

Goal Setting: Bezos set specific, measurable goals such as expanding Amazon's product offerings, improving customer experience, and increasing market share. Each goal was aligned with his vision of making Amazon the world's leading online retailer.

Prioritization: Bezos prioritized tasks that directly contributed to customer satisfaction and long-term growth. He focused on innovation, efficient logistics, and customer service, delegating other tasks to his team. By prioritizing these critical areas, Amazon grew from an online bookstore to a global e-commerce giant.

Example: Sara Blakely and Spanx

Sara Blakely, the founder of Spanx, built her business from the ground up with a clear vision and effective prioritization. Her vision was to create comfortable, flattering shapewear for women, which guided her goal setting and daily tasks.

Goal Setting: Blakely set SMART goals such as developing a product prototype, securing a manufacturing partner, and launching a marketing campaign. Each goal was specific, measurable, achievable, relevant, and time-bound.

Prioritization: Blakely prioritized tasks that directly impacted product development and market entry. She focused on creating a high-quality product, pitching to potential investors, and building brand awareness. By prioritizing these key areas, Spanx quickly became a household name in the fashion industry.

Implementing Goal Setting and Prioritization in Your Business

To implement effective goal setting and prioritization in your business, follow these steps:

1. **Define Your Vision and Mission**: Clearly articulate your business's long-term vision and mission. Ensure they are inspiring, focused, and aligned with your values.

2. **Set SMART Goals:** Use the SMART criteria to set specific, measurable, achievable, relevant, and time-bound goals that align with your vision and mission.

3. **Prioritize Tasks:** Use techniques like the Eisenhower Matrix, the ABCDE Method, or the Ivy Lee Method to prioritize tasks based on their urgency and importance.

4. **Regularly Review and Adjust:** circumstances and new opportunities. Continuously review your goals and priorities to ensure they remain aligned with your vision and mission. Adjust them as needed based on changing

5. **Communicate Clearly:** Ensure your team understands the vision, mission, goals, and priorities. Clear communication helps align everyone's efforts and fosters a sense of shared purpose.

6. **Stay Focused and Disciplined:** Maintain focus on your high-priority tasks and avoid distractions. Discipline is key to achieving your goals and driving business success.

Conclusion

Setting clear goals and priorities is fundamental to entrepreneurial success. By defining a compelling vision and mission, setting SMART goals, and prioritizing tasks effectively, entrepreneurs can ensure they are working on what truly matters. These practices not only enhance productivity and efficiency but also provide a clear direction and purpose for the business.

Remember, successful entrepreneurs like Jeff Bezos and Sara Blakely have demonstrated the power of clear goals and effective prioritization. By implementing these strategies in your own business, you can achieve your objectives, drive growth, and realize your entrepreneurial vision.

Chapter 3: Planning and Scheduling

Creating a Daily Schedule

An effective daily schedule is crucial for maximizing productivity and ensuring that you focus on tasks that contribute to your goals. A well-designed schedule helps you manage your time efficiently, reduce stress, and maintain a balance between work and personal life. Here are some tips for creating an effective daily schedule:

Understand Your Peak Productivity Times

Everyone has different times of the day when they are most productive. Identify when you are most alert and focused—this is when you should schedule your most important and demanding tasks.

Steps to Identify Peak Productivity Times:

1. **Track Your Energy Levels**: For a week, note down when you feel most energetic and when you feel sluggish.
2. **Analyze Patterns**: Look for patterns in your energy levels. Are you more productive in the morning, afternoon, or evening?
3. **Adjust Accordingly**: Schedule your high-priority tasks during your peak productivity times and less demanding tasks during low-energy periods.

Prioritize Your Tasks

Use prioritization techniques such as the Eisenhower Matrix or the ABCDE Method (discussed in Chapter 2) to identify the most important tasks to complete each day. Focus on high-priority tasks that align with your goals and contribute to your long-term success.

Steps to Prioritize Tasks:

1. **List All Tasks**: Write down all the tasks you need to complete.
2. **Categorize and Prioritize**: Use a prioritization method to categorize and rank tasks by importance and urgency.
3. **Focus on Top Priorities**: Ensure that your daily schedule includes time blocks for your highest-priority tasks.

Set Realistic Time Frames

Assign realistic time frames to each task based on your experience and the complexity of the task. Overestimating how much you can accomplish in a day can lead to stress and burnout.

Steps to Set Realistic Time Frames:

1. **Estimate Time Required**: Based on past experiences, estimate the time needed for each task.

2. **Buffer Time**: Include buffer time between tasks to account for unforeseen delays.
3. **Review and Adjust**: Regularly review your schedule to see if your time estimates are accurate and adjust as needed.

Use a Digital or Physical Planner

Choose a planning tool that works best for you, whether it's a digital app or a physical planner. Digital tools often offer features such as reminders, syncing across devices, and analytics, while physical planners can be more flexible and personalized.

Popular Digital Planning Tools:

- **Trello**: A visual tool for organizing tasks and projects using boards, lists, and cards.
- **Google Calendar**: A versatile calendar app that integrates with other Google services and allows for easy scheduling and reminders.
- **Todoist**: A task management app that helps you organize tasks, set deadlines, and track progress.

Physical Planner Tips:

- **Daily Planner**: Choose a planner with daily pages to write down detailed schedules and to-do lists.
- **Bullet Journal**: Create a customized planning system using a blank notebook, combining calendars, to-do lists, and goal-setting tools.

Review and Reflect

At the end of each day, review what you have accomplished and reflect on what worked well and what didn't. This helps you refine your scheduling process and continuously improve your productivity.

Steps for Daily Review and Reflection:

1. **Check Off Completed Tasks**: Mark tasks that you completed during the day.
2. **Analyze Unfinished Tasks**: Identify tasks that you didn't complete and understand why.
3. **Plan for Tomorrow**: Adjust your schedule for the next day based on today's experience.

Using Time Blocks

Time blocking is a powerful time management technique that involves dividing your day into blocks of time, each dedicated to a specific task or activity. This method helps you maintain focus, avoid multitasking, and ensure that you allocate sufficient time for important activities.

What is Time Blocking?

Time blocking is the practice of scheduling specific blocks of time for different tasks or activities throughout your day. Each block is dedicated to one task or a group of related tasks, allowing you to concentrate fully on the activity at hand without interruptions.

Benefits of Time Blocking:

- **Improved Focus**: By dedicating time blocks to specific tasks, you can concentrate better and avoid distractions.
- **Enhanced Productivity**: Time blocking helps you work more efficiently by providing a structured approach to your day.
- **Better Time Management**: This technique ensures that you allocate enough time for important tasks and reduces the likelihood of procrastination.

How to Implement Time Blocking

Implementing time blocking requires careful planning and discipline. Here are the steps to get started:

1. **List Your Tasks**: Write down all the tasks you need to accomplish for the day or week.
2. **Categorize Tasks**: Group similar tasks together to create blocks for related activities.
3. **Allocate Time Blocks**: Assign specific time blocks to each task or group of tasks based on their priority and estimated completion time.
4. **Schedule Breaks**: Include breaks between time blocks to rest and recharge.
5. **Stick to the Schedule**: Follow your time blocks as closely as possible, adjusting only when necessary.

Example Time Blocking Schedule:

Time	Task
8:00 - 9:00 AM	Morning routine and planning
9:00 - 11:00 AM	Project A: Research and development
11:00 - 11:15 AM	Break
11:15 AM - 1:00 PM	Client meetings and follow-ups
1:00 - 1:30 PM	Lunch
1:30 - 3:00 PM	Marketing strategy planning
3:00 - 3:15 PM	Break
3:15 - 5:00 PM	Administrative tasks and emails
5:00 - 6:00 PM	Exercise or personal time
6:00 - 7:00 PM	Dinner
7:00 - 9:00 PM	Evening routine and personal projects

Combining Time Blocking with Other Techniques

Time blocking can be combined with other time management techniques for even greater effectiveness. Here are some examples:

Pomodoro Technique: Combine time blocking with the Pomodoro Technique by breaking down time blocks into smaller intervals (typically 25 minutes of work followed by a 5-minute break).

Example: During a 2-hour time block for research, you can use four Pomodoro intervals (25 minutes of focused work + 5 minutes of break).

Batching: Group similar tasks together within a time block to minimize context switching and increase efficiency.

Example: Dedicate a 2-hour time block to handle all administrative tasks, such as emails, scheduling, and paperwork.

Planning for the Unexpected

No matter how well you plan, unexpected events and interruptions are inevitable. Incorporating flexibility into your schedule allows you to handle these disruptions without derailing your entire day.

Building Buffer Time

Buffer time is the extra time you allocate between tasks or at the end of the day to accommodate unexpected delays or urgent tasks. This helps you stay on track even when things don't go as planned.

Steps to Build Buffer Time:

1. **Identify Potential Disruptions**: Consider common interruptions or delays that occur in your day.
2. **Allocate Extra Time**: Add buffer time between tasks or at specific points in your schedule.
3. **Use Wisely**: Use buffer time for urgent tasks, or as an opportunity to catch up on delayed tasks.

Flexible Scheduling

A flexible schedule allows for adjustments and changes without compromising productivity. This involves having a plan but being open to re-prioritizing tasks as needed.

Steps for Flexible Scheduling:

1. **Set Core Hours**: Identify core hours where you focus on high-priority tasks.
2. **Leave Open Slots**: Keep some time slots open for unexpected tasks or opportunities.
3. **Adjust Daily**: Review and adjust your schedule at the start and end of each day based on new developments.

Contingency Planning

Contingency planning involves having backup plans for critical tasks or projects. This ensures that you can still meet your goals even when unexpected events occur.

Steps for Contingency Planning:

1. **Identify Critical Tasks**: Determine which tasks or projects are most crucial to your business.
2. **Create Backup Plans**: Develop alternative plans or solutions for these tasks in case of disruptions.
3. **Communicate Plans**: Ensure your team is aware of contingency plans and knows how to implement them if needed.

Real-World Examples of Planning and Scheduling

To illustrate the principles of effective planning and scheduling, let's look at some real-world examples of entrepreneurs who excel in these areas:

Example: Elon Musk

Elon Musk, CEO of Tesla and SpaceX, is known for his rigorous time management and planning. He uses time blocking to manage his schedule down to five-minute intervals, ensuring he allocates time efficiently across his various responsibilities.

Planning and Scheduling Practices:

- **Time Blocking**: Musk's days are divided into precise time blocks, allowing him to focus on specific tasks without distraction.
- **Prioritization**: He prioritizes high-impact tasks and projects that align with his long-term vision for his companies.
- **Flexibility**: Despite his rigorous schedule, Musk remains adaptable, adjusting his plans as needed to address urgent matters.

Example: Sheryl Sandberg

Sheryl Sandberg, COO of Facebook, is known for her structured approach to time management. She emphasizes the importance of a daily routine and effective scheduling to balance her professional and personal life.

Planning and Scheduling Practices:

- **Daily Routine**: Sandberg follows a consistent daily routine that includes

time for planning, meetings, and personal activities.

- **Prioritization**: She prioritizes tasks that contribute to her key goals and ensures her schedule reflects these priorities.

- **Buffer Time**: Sandberg builds buffer time into her schedule to handle unexpected events and maintain balance.

Implementing Effective Planning and Scheduling in Your Business

To implement effective planning and scheduling in your business, follow these steps:

1. **Create a Daily Schedule**: Design a daily schedule that aligns with your peak productivity times and priorities. Use digital or physical planning tools that suit your preferences.

2. **Use Time Blocks**: Implement time blocking to allocate specific periods for different tasks or activities. Combine time blocking with other techniques like the Pomodoro Technique or batching for greater efficiency.

3. **Plan for the Unexpected**: Incorporate buffer time and flexibility into your schedule to handle interruptions and urgent tasks. Develop contingency plans for critical projects to ensure you can stay on track even when disruptions occur.

4. **Regularly Review and Adjust**: Continuously review and adjust your schedule based on your experiences and changing circumstances. Use daily reflection to identify areas for improvement

and make necessary adjustments.

5. **Communicate Clearly**: Ensure your team understands the importance of planning and scheduling and how it contributes to overall productivity. Encourage them to adopt similar practices to enhance their efficiency.

6. **Stay Disciplined**: Maintain discipline in following your schedule and time blocks. Avoid distractions and stay focused on the task at hand to maximize productivity.

Conclusion

Effective planning and scheduling are essential for entrepreneurial success. By creating a daily schedule, using time blocks, and planning for the unexpected, entrepreneurs can manage their time efficiently, increase productivity, and achieve their business goals.

Remember, successful entrepreneurs like Elon Musk and Sheryl Sandberg demonstrate the power of rigorous planning and scheduling. By implementing these strategies in your own business, you can enhance your productivity, stay on track, and realize your entrepreneurial vision.

Chapter 4: Leveraging Technology for Efficiency

Tools for Time Management

In today's fast-paced business environment, leveraging technology for time management is crucial for staying organized, productive, and efficient. Numerous tools and apps are available to help entrepreneurs manage their time effectively, streamline their workflows, and achieve their goals. This section will explore some of the most popular and useful time management tools and apps.

Calendar Apps

Calendar apps are essential for scheduling and organizing your time. They help you keep track of appointments, deadlines, and events, ensuring you never miss important dates.

Popular Calendar Apps:

1. **Google Calendar**: A versatile and user-friendly calendar app that integrates seamlessly with other Google services. It allows you to schedule events, set reminders, and share calendars with team members.

    - **Features**: Multiple calendar views (day, week, month), event reminders, integration with Gmail, and collaboration tools.

- **Link**: Google Calendar
2. **Microsoft Outlook Calendar**: Part of the Microsoft Office suite, Outlook Calendar is ideal for professionals who use Microsoft Office tools. It offers robust scheduling features and integrates with email and other Office applications.

    - **Features**: Email integration, meeting scheduling, shared calendars, and mobile app support.
    - **Link**: Outlook Calendar
3. **Apple Calendar**: A built-in calendar app for macOS and iOS devices. It syncs across Apple devices and integrates with iCloud, making it easy to access your schedule on the go.

    - **Features**: Natural language input, event alerts, iCloud integration, and collaboration features.
    - **Link**: Apple Calendar

Task Management Apps

Task management apps help you organize and prioritize your to-do lists, ensuring you stay on top of your tasks and deadlines.

Popular Task Management Apps:

1. **Todoist**: A powerful task management app that helps you organize tasks, set deadlines, and track progress. It supports various productivity

methodologies like GTD (Getting Things Done).

    - **Features**: Task categorization, due dates, reminders, project management, and collaboration tools.
    - **Link**: Todoist
2. **Trello**: A visual project management tool that uses boards, lists, and cards to help you organize tasks and projects. Trello is highly customizable and suitable for both personal and team use.

    - **Features**: Drag-and-drop interface, customizable boards, task assignments, and integration with other apps.
    - **Link**: Trello
3. **Asana**: A comprehensive task and project management app designed for teams. It allows you to create tasks, assign them to team members, and track progress in real-time.

    - **Features**: Task assignments, project timelines, collaboration tools, and workflow automation.
    - **Link**: Asana

Time Tracking Apps

Time tracking apps help you monitor how you spend your time, allowing you to identify areas where you can improve efficiency.

Popular Time Tracking Apps:

1. **Toggl**: A simple and intuitive time tracking app that helps you track work hours and analyze productivity. Toggl offers detailed reports and integrates with various project management tools.

   - **Features**: One-click time tracking, detailed reports, project tracking, and integration with other tools.
   - **Link**: Toggl

2. **Harvest**: A time tracking and invoicing app designed for freelancers and small businesses. Harvest allows you to track time, manage projects, and generate invoices based on tracked hours.

   - **Features**: Time tracking, expense tracking, invoicing, and integration with other productivity tools.
   - **Link**: Harvest

3. **Clockify**: A free time tracking app that helps you monitor work hours, manage projects, and improve productivity. Clockify offers both manual and automatic time tracking options.

   - **Features**: Time tracking, project management, detailed reports, and team collaboration tools.
   - **Link**: Clockify

Automating Repetitive Tasks

Automating repetitive tasks is an effective way to save time and reduce the risk of human error. By leveraging technology to handle routine activities, you can focus on more strategic and value-added tasks. This section explores various ways to automate repetitive tasks.

Workflow Automation Tools

Workflow automation tools allow you to create automated workflows that perform tasks and processes without manual intervention.

Popular Workflow Automation Tools:

1. **Zapier**: A powerful automation tool that connects different apps and services to create automated workflows (called "Zaps"). Zapier supports thousands of apps, making it highly versatile.

    - **Features**: App integration, multi-step workflows, conditional logic, and real-time automation.
    - **Link**: Zapier
2. **Integromat (now Make)**: An advanced automation platform that allows you to connect apps and automate complex workflows. Integromat supports various data transformations and integrations.

- **Features**: Visual workflow builder, app integration, data manipulation, and error handling.
- **Link**: Make (formerly Integromat)
3. **Microsoft Power Automate**: Part of the Microsoft Power Platform, Power Automate enables you to create automated workflows between your favorite apps and services. It's ideal for businesses using Microsoft Office tools.

    - **Features**: App integration, workflow templates, business process automation, and AI capabilities.
    - **Link**: Power Automate

Email Automation

Email automation helps you manage and streamline your email communications, saving time and ensuring timely responses.

Popular Email Automation Tools:

1. **Mailchimp**: A widely-used email marketing platform that allows you to automate email campaigns, send personalized messages, and track engagement metrics.

    - **Features**: Email templates, audience segmentation, automation workflows, and analytics.
    - **Link**: Mailchimp

2. **ActiveCampaign**: An email marketing and automation tool that helps you create targeted email campaigns, automate follow-ups, and track customer interactions.

    - **Features**: Email automation, CRM integration, lead scoring, and reporting.
    - **Link**: ActiveCampaign
3. **HubSpot**: A comprehensive marketing, sales, and service platform that offers robust email automation features. HubSpot helps you manage your entire customer journey with automation.

    - **Features**: Email automation, CRM, lead nurturing, and analytics.
    - **Link**: HubSpot

Social Media Automation

Social media automation tools help you schedule posts, manage multiple accounts, and analyze performance, ensuring consistent and efficient social media management.

Popular Social Media Automation Tools:

1. **Buffer**: A social media scheduling tool that allows you to plan and schedule posts across multiple platforms. Buffer provides analytics to help you measure the success of your posts.

- **Features**: Post scheduling, social media analytics, team collaboration, and engagement tracking.
- **Link**: Buffer
2. **Hootsuite**: A comprehensive social media management platform that enables you to schedule posts, manage multiple accounts, and analyze performance metrics.

    - **Features**: Post scheduling, social media monitoring, analytics, and team collaboration.
    - **Link**: Hootsuite
3. **Later**: A visual social media scheduling tool that is particularly popular for Instagram. Later allows you to plan, schedule, and analyze your social media content.

    - **Features**: Visual content calendar, post scheduling, media library, and analytics.
    - **Link**: Later

Managing Communication and Collaboration

Effective communication and collaboration are essential for any business. Using the right tools can enhance productivity, streamline workflows, and ensure that everyone stays connected and informed. This section explores tips and tools for managing communication and collaboration effectively.

Communication Tools

Communication tools help you stay connected with your team, clients, and stakeholders. They facilitate real-time communication, file sharing, and collaboration.

Popular Communication Tools:

1. **Slack**: A team communication platform that offers real-time messaging, file sharing, and integrations with other productivity tools. Slack's channels and direct messaging features help keep communication organized.

    - **Features**: Channels, direct messaging, file sharing, integrations, and video calls.
    - **Link**: Slack
2. **Microsoft Teams**: A collaboration platform that integrates with Microsoft Office 365, offering chat, video conferencing, file sharing, and project management features.

    - **Features**: Chat, video calls, file sharing, Office 365 integration, and collaboration tools.
    - **Link**: Microsoft Teams
3. **Zoom**: A video conferencing tool that enables virtual meetings, webinars, and team collaboration. Zoom is known for its high-quality video and audio capabilities.

    - **Features**: Video conferencing, screen sharing, webinar hosting, and recording.

- **Link**: Zoom

Collaboration Tools

Collaboration tools help teams work together more efficiently, manage projects, and share information seamlessly.

Popular Collaboration Tools:

1. **Trello**

: A visual project management tool that uses boards, lists, and cards to organize tasks and projects. Trello's collaborative features make it easy to work with team members.

- **Features**: Boards, lists, cards, task assignments, and integrations.
- **Link**: Trello
2. **Asana**: A project management tool that helps teams organize tasks, track progress, and collaborate on projects. Asana offers various views, such as lists, boards, and timelines.
    - **Features**: Task assignments, project timelines, team collaboration, and workflow automation.
    - **Link**: Asana
3. **Google Workspace**: A suite of productivity and collaboration tools that includes Gmail, Google Drive, Docs, Sheets, and more. Google Workspace

allows teams to collaborate in real-time on documents and projects.

- **Features**: Real-time collaboration, file sharing, email, and calendar integration.
- **Link**: Google Workspace

Best Practices for Managing Communication and Collaboration

To make the most of communication and collaboration tools, it's important to follow best practices that enhance productivity and ensure smooth workflows.

1. **Set Clear Communication Guidelines**: Establish guidelines for how and when to use different communication channels (e.g., email for formal communication, Slack for quick messages).
2. **Use Channels and Groups**: Organize communication by creating channels or groups for specific projects or topics. This helps keep discussions focused and relevant.
3. **Schedule Regular Check-Ins**: Hold regular team meetings or check-ins to discuss progress, address issues, and keep everyone aligned.
4. **Leverage Collaboration Features**: Use features like task assignments, file sharing, and real-time editing to facilitate collaboration and ensure everyone has access to the necessary information.
5. **Encourage Transparency**: Promote transparency by sharing updates, progress, and challenges with

the team. This helps build trust and ensures everyone is on the same page.
6. **Monitor and Adjust**: Regularly review your communication and collaboration processes to identify areas for improvement and make necessary adjustments.

Integrating Tools for Maximum Efficiency

Integrating different tools can enhance efficiency by creating a seamless workflow across various tasks and processes. Many tools offer integrations with other apps, allowing you to automate processes and streamline your work.

Examples of Tool Integrations

1. **Trello and Slack**: Integrate Trello with Slack to receive updates and notifications about project progress directly in your Slack channels. This helps keep everyone informed without switching between apps.

    - **Integration Link**: Trello and Slack Integration
2. **Asana and Google Calendar**: Sync Asana tasks with Google Calendar to see your tasks and deadlines alongside your calendar events. This integration helps you manage your time more effectively.

- **Integration Link**: Asana and Google Calendar Integration
3. **Zapier Integrations**: Use Zapier to connect various apps and create custom workflows. For example, you can create a Zap that automatically adds new email subscribers to your CRM or sends Slack notifications for new Trello cards.

    - **Integration Link**: Zapier Integrations

Real-World Examples of Leveraging Technology for Efficiency

To illustrate how technology can enhance efficiency, let's look at some real-world examples of entrepreneurs and businesses that successfully leverage technology.

Example: Buffer

Buffer is a social media management platform that has grown significantly by leveraging technology for efficiency. The Buffer team uses various tools to streamline their workflows and enhance productivity.

Tools and Practices Used:

- **Trello**: Buffer uses Trello for project management and collaboration. The team organizes tasks and projects using boards, lists, and cards, ensuring everyone stays aligned and informed.
- **Slack**: For team communication, Buffer relies on Slack. Channels are created for different projects

and topics, facilitating focused and organized discussions.
- **Zoom**: Buffer conducts virtual meetings and webinars using Zoom. This allows team members to connect and collaborate regardless of their location.
- **Zapier**: Buffer automates various workflows using Zapier. For example, they use Zaps to automate tasks like sending social media updates or syncing data between apps.

Example: Automattic

Automattic, the company behind WordPress.com, has a fully distributed workforce and relies heavily on technology for communication and collaboration. The company uses various tools to ensure smooth workflows and maintain productivity.

Tools and Practices Used:

- **Slack**: Automattic uses Slack for team communication. Channels are created for different teams and projects, and integrations with other tools help streamline workflows.
- **Zoom**: For virtual meetings and team check-ins, Automattic uses Zoom. This helps maintain strong communication and collaboration among remote team members.
- **P2 (WordPress Theme)**: Automattic developed P2, a WordPress theme designed for team collaboration. P2 allows team members to share

updates, discuss projects, and collaborate asynchronously.
- **Google Workspace**: Automattic uses Google Workspace for email, document collaboration, and file sharing. This ensures that all team members have access to the necessary tools and information.

Implementing Technology for Efficiency in Your Business

To implement technology for efficiency in your business, follow these steps:

1. **Identify Your Needs**: Determine the specific needs and challenges of your business. Consider areas where technology can help streamline processes and enhance productivity.
2. **Choose the Right Tools**: Select tools and apps that align with your business needs. Consider factors like ease of use, features, integrations, and cost.
3. **Integrate Tools**: Look for opportunities to integrate different tools to create a seamless workflow. Use platforms like Zapier to connect apps and automate processes.
4. **Train Your Team**: Ensure your team is familiar with the tools and knows how to use them effectively. Provide training and resources to help them get up to speed.

5. **Monitor and Optimize**: Regularly review your use of technology and make adjustments as needed. Look for new tools and features that can further enhance efficiency.

Conclusion

Leveraging technology for efficiency is essential for modern entrepreneurs. By using tools for time management, automating repetitive tasks, and managing communication and collaboration effectively, you can save time, reduce stress, and focus on strategic activities that drive business success.

Remember, successful entrepreneurs and businesses like Buffer and Automattic demonstrate the power of technology in enhancing productivity. By implementing these strategies in your own business, you can streamline your workflows, stay organized, and achieve your entrepreneurial goals.

Chapter 5: Delegating and Outsourcing

Understanding What to Delegate

Effective delegation and outsourcing are critical skills for entrepreneurs. Knowing what tasks to delegate can free up your time for high-impact activities, improve productivity, and enhance the overall efficiency of your business. This section will explore the criteria for determining which tasks to delegate and how to make the most of delegation.

Criteria for Determining Tasks to Delegate

1. **Repetitiveness and Routine**: Tasks that are repetitive and routine can often be delegated. These tasks do not require high-level decision-making and can be easily performed by others with the right instructions.

    - **Examples**: Data entry, scheduling meetings, managing emails, and basic administrative tasks.
2. **Low Skill Requirements**: Tasks that do not require specialized skills or expertise can be delegated to less experienced team members or outsourced to virtual assistants.

- **Examples**: Social media posting, basic customer support, and research.
3. **Time-Consuming Activities**: Tasks that consume a significant amount of your time but do not contribute directly to your core responsibilities should be considered for delegation.

    - **Examples**: Travel arrangements, document formatting, and maintaining databases.
4. **Specialized Tasks Outside Your Expertise**: Tasks that require skills or knowledge you do not possess should be delegated to experts. This ensures the task is completed efficiently and to a high standard.

    - **Examples**: Graphic design, web development, legal work, and accounting.
5. **Tasks That Others Can Do Better**: Identify tasks that others can perform better than you due to their specific skills or experience. Delegating these tasks can lead to better outcomes and free you up to focus on your strengths.

    - **Examples**: Content creation, marketing strategy, and technical support.
6. **Tasks That Support Business Growth**: Tasks that contribute to the growth and scalability of your business should be delegated to ensure they receive the attention and resources they need.

- **Examples**: Lead generation, sales outreach, and market research.

Benefits of Delegating Tasks

1. **Increased Efficiency**: By delegating tasks, you can focus on high-priority activities that require your attention, thereby increasing overall efficiency and productivity.
2. **Better Time Management**: Delegation helps you manage your time more effectively, allowing you to allocate more time to strategic planning and decision-making.
3. **Skill Development**: Delegating tasks to your team members provides them with opportunities to develop new skills and take on more responsibilities.
4. **Improved Focus**: By offloading routine tasks, you can concentrate on activities that align with your core competencies and business goals.
5. **Scalability**: Delegation is essential for scaling your business. It enables you to expand your operations without becoming overwhelmed by day-to-day tasks.

Finding the Right People

Once you've identified the tasks to delegate, the next step is finding the right people to take on these responsibilities. This involves hiring employees, contracting freelancers, or outsourcing to specialized service providers.

Hiring Employees

Hiring full-time or part-time employees can be an effective way to delegate tasks and build a dedicated team. Here's how to find the right people:

1. **Define the Role**: Clearly outline the responsibilities, qualifications, and skills required for the role. This will help you attract suitable candidates.

    - **Example Job Description**: "Seeking a detail-oriented administrative assistant to manage scheduling, emails, and customer support. Must have excellent communication skills and proficiency in Microsoft Office."
2. **Recruitment Channels**: Use various recruitment channels to reach potential candidates. This includes job boards, company websites, social media, and employee referrals.

    - **Popular Job Boards**: Indeed, LinkedIn, Glassdoor, Monster
3. **Screening and Interviewing**: Screen resumes and conduct interviews to assess candidates' qualifications, experience, and fit with your company culture. Use structured interviews and standardized questions to ensure fairness and

consistency.

- **Sample Interview Questions**: "Can you describe your experience with task management software?", "How do you prioritize multiple tasks with competing deadlines?"

4. **Skills Assessment**: Use skills assessments or practical tests to evaluate candidates' abilities. This can help you determine if they have the necessary skills to perform the tasks effectively.

    - **Skills Assessment Tools**: TestGorilla, HackerRank

5. **Reference Checks**: Conduct reference checks to verify candidates' work history, performance, and reliability. Speak with former employers or colleagues to get a comprehensive view of the candidate.

Contracting Freelancers

Freelancers offer flexibility and specialized skills for short-term projects or ongoing tasks. Here's how to find and hire freelancers:

1. **Freelance Platforms**: Use freelance platforms to find skilled professionals for various tasks. These platforms allow you to browse portfolios, read

reviews, and communicate with freelancers.

- **Popular Freelance Platforms**: Upwork, Fiverr, Toptal
2. **Clearly Define the Project**: Provide a detailed project description, including the scope, deliverables, timeline, and budget. Clear communication helps attract the right freelancers.

    - **Sample Project Description**: "Looking for a graphic designer to create a logo and branding materials for a new product launch. Must have experience with Adobe Illustrator and a portfolio of previous work."
3. **Review Portfolios and Proposals**: Evaluate freelancers' portfolios and proposals to assess their skills, experience, and understanding of the project. Look for relevant experience and high-quality work.

    -
    -
    -
    - **Proposal Evaluation Criteria**: Relevant experience, quality of previous work, understanding of the project, and proposed timeline and budget.
4. **Conduct Interviews**: Interview shortlisted freelancers to discuss the project in detail, assess their communication skills, and ensure they are a

good fit for your needs.

- ○ **Sample Interview Questions**: "How do you handle tight deadlines?", "Can you describe a similar project you have completed?"
5. **Set Clear Expectations**: Clearly outline your expectations, milestones, and communication plan. Use contracts or agreements to formalize the terms and protect both parties.

    - ○ **Contract Elements**: Project scope, deliverables, timeline, payment terms, and confidentiality clauses.

Outsourcing to Service Providers

Outsourcing to specialized service providers can help you access expert skills and resources for tasks that are outside your core competencies. Here's how to find and manage outsourcing partners:

1. **Identify Service Providers**: Research and identify service providers that specialize in the tasks you want to outsource. Look for providers with a proven track record and positive reviews.

    - ○ **Examples of Outsourcing Services**: IT support, digital marketing, customer service, accounting, and legal services.
2. **Evaluate Credentials and Experience**: Assess the credentials, experience, and reputation of

potential service providers. Request case studies, client testimonials, and references to verify their expertise.

- **Evaluation Criteria**: Industry experience, client feedback, service quality, and cost-effectiveness.

3. **Request Proposals**: Request detailed proposals from shortlisted service providers. Compare their offerings, pricing, and approach to determine the best fit for your needs.

- **Proposal Elements**: Service description, methodology, timeline, pricing, and references.

4. **Conduct Due Diligence**: Perform due diligence by checking references, verifying credentials, and assessing financial stability. Ensure the provider has the necessary resources to deliver on their promises.

- **Due Diligence Steps**: Reference checks, financial assessments, and site visits (if applicable).

5. **Negotiate and Formalize Agreements**: Negotiate terms and conditions, including service level agreements (SLAs), performance metrics, and payment terms. Use contracts to formalize the relationship and protect both parties.

- **Contract Elements**: Scope of work, performance metrics, payment terms, confidentiality, and termination clauses.

Managing Outsourced Tasks

Effective management of outsourced tasks is essential to ensure quality and efficiency. This section provides best practices for managing and monitoring outsourced tasks.

Establish Clear Communication

1. **Set Communication Channels**: Establish clear communication channels for regular updates, feedback, and issue resolution. Use tools like email, instant messaging, and video conferencing to stay connected.

    - **Communication Tools**: Slack, Microsoft Teams, Zoom, email.
2. **Define Communication Protocols**: Set communication protocols, including frequency of updates, preferred communication methods, and response times. Ensure all parties are aware of and adhere to these protocols.

    - **Example Protocols**: Weekly progress reports, bi-weekly video calls, 24-hour response time for urgent issues.
3. **Designate Points of Contact**: Designate points of contact for both your business and the service

provider. This ensures clear accountability and facilitates efficient communication.

- **Example Points of Contact**: Project manager, account manager, technical lead.

Monitor Performance and Quality

1. **Set Performance Metrics**: Define performance metrics and key performance indicators (KPIs) to measure the success of outsourced tasks. Use these metrics to track progress and ensure quality.

    - **Example KPIs**: Project completion time, error rate, customer satisfaction, and cost savings.

2. **Regularly Review Progress**: Conduct regular progress reviews to assess the performance of the service provider. Use these reviews to provide feedback, address issues, and make necessary adjustments.

    - **Review Frequency**: Weekly progress meetings, monthly performance reviews, quarterly strategic reviews.

3. **Conduct Quality Assurance Checks**: Implement quality assurance (QA) checks to ensure the work meets your standards and requirements. Use QA processes to

identify and address any quality issues promptly.

- **QA Processes**: Regular audits, random spot checks, and user acceptance testing.
4. **Provide Constructive Feedback**: Provide constructive feedback to the service provider to help them improve their performance. Recognize achievements and address areas for improvement.
    - **Feedback Techniques**: Specific, timely, and actionable feedback; regular feedback sessions.

Mitigate Risks and Manage Issues

1. **Identify Potential Risks**: Identify potential risks associated with outsourcing, such as quality issues, delays, and communication breakdowns. Develop strategies to mitigate these risks.

    - **Risk Mitigation Strategies**: Contingency planning, risk assessments, and backup plans.
2. **Develop a Contingency Plan**: Develop a contingency plan to address potential issues that may arise. This plan should include steps to take in case of service disruptions, quality problems, or other risks.

    - **Contingency Plan Elements**: Alternative providers, escalation procedures, and crisis management protocols.

3. **Resolve Issues Promptly**: Address any issues that arise promptly and effectively. Use a structured approach to problem-solving and involve the necessary stakeholders to find solutions.

    - **Issue Resolution Steps**: Identify the issue, analyze the cause, develop a solution, and implement corrective actions.
4. **Evaluate and Adjust**: Regularly evaluate the outsourcing relationship and make adjustments as needed. This includes assessing performance, reviewing contracts, and considering changes to the scope of work.

    - **Evaluation Frequency**: Annual reviews, periodic contract assessments, and ad-hoc evaluations.

Real-World Examples of Effective Delegation and Outsourcing

To illustrate the power of delegation and outsourcing, let's look at some real-world examples of businesses that have successfully implemented these strategies.

Example: Basecamp

Basecamp, a project management and team collaboration software company, has effectively utilized delegation and outsourcing to grow its business.

Delegation and Outsourcing Practices:

- **Customer Support**: Basecamp outsources part of its customer support to ensure 24/7 availability and high-quality service. This allows the in-house team to focus on product development and strategic initiatives.
- **Content Creation**: The company delegates content creation, such as blog posts and marketing materials, to freelance writers and content agencies. This ensures a steady stream of high-quality content without overburdening the internal team.
- **Software Development**: Basecamp delegates specific development tasks to specialized software development firms. This enables the company to leverage expert skills and accelerate product development.

Example: Slack

Slack, a popular team communication tool, leverages delegation and outsourcing to manage its rapid growth and maintain high standards of service.

Delegation and Outsourcing Practices:

- **IT and Infrastructure**: Slack outsources its IT infrastructure management to cloud service providers like Amazon Web Services (AWS). This allows Slack to scale its services efficiently and focus on core product innovation.

- **Localization**: To cater to a global audience, Slack outsources localization and translation services to specialized agencies. This ensures that the platform is accessible and user-friendly for users in different regions.
- **Marketing and PR**: Slack delegates various marketing and public relations tasks to external agencies. These agencies handle media relations, campaign management, and content creation, enabling Slack to maintain a strong market presence.

Implementing Delegation and Outsourcing in Your Business

To implement delegation and outsourcing effectively in your business, follow these steps:

1. **Assess Your Needs**: Identify the tasks that can be delegated or outsourced based on the criteria discussed earlier. Consider the potential benefits and challenges of delegating each task.
2. **Create a Plan**: Develop a detailed plan for delegation and outsourcing, including the tasks to be delegated, the criteria for selecting candidates or service providers, and the timeline for implementation.
3. **Select the Right People or Partners**: Use the guidelines provided to find and hire the right employees, freelancers, or service providers.

Ensure they have the necessary skills and experience to perform the tasks effectively.
4. **Set Clear Expectations**: Communicate your expectations clearly, including the scope of work, deadlines, performance metrics, and communication protocols. Use contracts or agreements to formalize these expectations.
5. **Monitor and Manage**: Regularly monitor the performance of delegated tasks and outsourced services. Provide feedback, conduct quality assurance checks, and address any issues promptly.
6. **Evaluate and Adjust**: Continuously evaluate the effectiveness of your delegation and outsourcing strategy. Make adjustments as needed to ensure ongoing success and efficiency.

Conclusion

Delegation and outsourcing are powerful strategies for entrepreneurs looking to free up their time and focus on high-impact activities. By understanding what tasks to delegate, finding the right people, and managing outsourced tasks effectively, you can enhance your productivity, improve efficiency, and drive business growth.

Implementing these strategies requires careful planning, clear communication, and ongoing management. However, the benefits of delegation and outsourcing far outweigh the challenges, making them essential tools for any entrepreneur aiming to build a successful and scalable business.

By learning from real-world examples and following best practices, you can leverage delegation and outsourcing to achieve your entrepreneurial goals and take your business to new heights.

Chapter 6: Minimizing Distractions and Staying Focused

Identifying Common Distractions

For entrepreneurs, distractions can significantly impact productivity and hinder the progress of their business goals. Understanding common distractions and their effects is the first step toward minimizing them and creating a more focused work environment.

Common Distractions Entrepreneurs Face

1. **Digital Distractions**

    - **Social Media**: Platforms like Facebook, Twitter, Instagram, and LinkedIn can be significant time-wasters. Notifications and the urge to check updates frequently can interrupt work and reduce productivity.
    - **Emails**: Constant email notifications and the need to respond to messages can be distracting. Sorting through spam and unnecessary emails can consume valuable time.
    - **Instant Messaging**: Tools like Slack, WhatsApp, and other chat applications can lead to frequent interruptions from colleagues, clients, or partners.

2. **Environmental Distractions**

    - **Noise**: Background noise from conversations, traffic, construction, or office equipment can be distracting and make it challenging to concentrate.
    - **Clutter**: A cluttered workspace can be visually distracting and can contribute to stress and disorganization.
    - **Interruptions**: Unexpected visits from colleagues, clients, or family members can disrupt focus and workflow.

3. **Internal Distractions**

    - **Multitasking**: Trying to juggle multiple tasks at once can lead to decreased efficiency and increased errors.
    - **Procrastination**: Delaying tasks can lead to rushed work and missed deadlines.
    - **Fatigue**: Lack of sleep, poor nutrition, or insufficient breaks can reduce concentration and productivity.

4. **Work-Life Balance Distractions**

    - **Family Responsibilities**: Entrepreneurs who work from home may face distractions from family members or household chores.
    - **Personal Issues**: Stress or preoccupation with personal problems can detract from work focus.

- **Overwork**: Long hours without adequate breaks can lead to burnout and decreased productivity.

Impact of Distractions on Productivity

1. **Reduced Efficiency**: Frequent distractions disrupt workflow, making it difficult to complete tasks efficiently and leading to longer work hours.
2. **Increased Errors**: Distractions can lead to mistakes, which require additional time and effort to correct.
3. **Decreased Creativity**: Constant interruptions can hinder creative thinking and problem-solving abilities.
4. **Higher Stress Levels**: Managing multiple distractions can increase stress and reduce overall job satisfaction.
5. **Lower Quality of Work**: A lack of focus can result in lower-quality work, which can impact business reputation and success.

Strategies to Stay Focused

Maintaining focus and improving concentration are essential for maximizing productivity and achieving business goals. Here are some effective strategies to help entrepreneurs stay focused:

Techniques to Maintain Focus

1. **Prioritize Tasks**

    - **Use the Eisenhower Matrix**: Categorize tasks into four quadrants based on urgency and importance to prioritize effectively.
        - **Quadrant 1**: Urgent and Important (Do immediately)
        - **Quadrant 2**: Important but Not Urgent (Schedule time to do)
        - **Quadrant 3**: Urgent but Not Important (Delegate)
        - **Quadrant 4**: Not Urgent and Not Important (Eliminate)
    - **Link**: Eisenhower Matrix

2. **Time Blocking**

    - **Schedule Dedicated Focus Time**: Allocate specific blocks of time for focused work without interruptions. Use a digital calendar to set these blocks.
    - **Pomodoro Technique**: Work in focused intervals (e.g., 25 minutes) followed by short breaks (e.g., 5 minutes) to maintain high levels of concentration.
    - **Link**: Pomodoro Technique

3. **Limit Digital Distractions**

- **Use Website Blockers**: Tools like StayFocusd, Freedom, and Cold Turkey can block distracting websites during work hours.
- **Turn Off Notifications**: Disable non-essential notifications on your phone and computer to minimize interruptions.
- **Designate Email Check Times**: Set specific times to check and respond to emails rather than constantly monitoring your inbox.

4. **Practice Mindfulness and Meditation**

    - **Mindfulness Techniques**: Practice mindfulness exercises to improve focus and reduce stress. Apps like Headspace and Calm offer guided meditations.
    - **Link**: Headspace, Calm

5. **Set Clear Goals and Deadlines**

    - **SMART Goals**: Use the SMART criteria (Specific, Measurable, Achievable, Relevant, Time-bound) to set clear and achievable goals.
    - **Daily and Weekly Goals**: Break down larger goals into daily and weekly tasks to maintain momentum and track progress.

6. **Take Regular Breaks**

    - **Scheduled Breaks**: Take regular breaks to rest and recharge. Short breaks (5-10

minutes) every hour can help maintain productivity.
- **Physical Activity**: Incorporate physical activity into your breaks to boost energy and focus.

Creating a Productive Work Environment

A well-designed work environment can significantly enhance focus and productivity. Here are tips for creating a workspace that minimizes distractions and promotes concentration:

1. **Optimize Your Workspace**

    - **Declutter**: Keep your workspace organized and free from unnecessary items. A tidy environment can reduce visual distractions and stress.
    - **Ergonomic Setup**: Use ergonomic furniture to ensure comfort and reduce physical strain. Adjust your chair, desk, and monitor to maintain proper posture.
    - **Adequate Lighting**: Ensure your workspace is well-lit. Natural light is ideal, but if that's not possible, use adequate artificial lighting to reduce eye strain.

2. **Minimize Noise**

    - **Noise-Canceling Headphones**: Use noise-canceling headphones to block out

background noise and create a quieter work environment.
- **White Noise Machines**: Consider using white noise machines or apps to mask distracting sounds.
- **Quiet Zones**: If possible, designate quiet zones in your workspace where interruptions are minimized.

3. **Create Boundaries**

   - **Physical Boundaries**: If you work from home, set up a dedicated workspace separate from common areas to minimize household distractions.
   - **Time Boundaries**: Establish specific work hours and communicate them to family members or housemates to minimize interruptions during work time.

4. **Personalize Your Space**

   - **Inspiring Decor**: Personalize your workspace with items that inspire and motivate you, such as plants, artwork, or motivational quotes.
   - **Comfortable Environment**: Ensure your workspace is comfortable, with appropriate temperature, ventilation, and seating.

5. **Utilize Productivity Tools**

- **Task Management Tools**: Use tools like Trello, Asana, or Todoist to organize tasks and track progress.
- **Calendar Apps**: Use digital calendars like Google Calendar or Outlook to schedule tasks, set reminders, and plan your day.
- **Focus Apps**: Apps like Focus@Will or Brain.fm provide music designed to enhance concentration and productivity.

6. **Implement a Routine**

    - **Daily Routine**: Establish a consistent daily routine to create structure and predictability. This can include regular start and end times, scheduled breaks, and planned tasks.
    - **Morning Rituals**: Start your day with a morning ritual that sets a positive tone, such as exercise, meditation, or planning your day.

Real-World Examples and Case Studies

To illustrate the effectiveness of these strategies, let's explore some real-world examples and case studies of entrepreneurs who have successfully minimized distractions and stayed focused:

Example 1: Elon Musk

Elon Musk, the CEO of Tesla and SpaceX, is known for his intense focus and productivity. Despite managing multiple high-profile companies, he uses several strategies to stay focused:

- **Time Blocking**: Musk is a strong advocate of time blocking. He divides his day into 5-minute slots, ensuring that he dedicates focused time to various tasks without wasting any.
- **Prioritization**: He prioritizes tasks based on their impact and importance, ensuring that his time is spent on high-leverage activities.
- **Limiting Meetings**: Musk minimizes the number of meetings he attends, especially if they do not add significant value to his work.

Example 2: Tim Ferriss

Tim Ferriss, the author of "The 4-Hour Workweek," emphasizes the importance of focus and efficiency. He employs several techniques to minimize distractions:

- **Batching Tasks**: Ferriss batches similar tasks together, such as checking emails at specific times rather than throughout the day, to minimize interruptions.
- **Selective Ignorance**: He practices selective ignorance by ignoring unnecessary information and focusing only on what is essential for his goals.
- **80/20 Principle**: Ferriss applies the Pareto Principle (80/20 Rule) to identify and focus on the 20% of activities that yield 80% of the results.

Example 3: Cal Newport

Cal Newport, the author of "Deep Work," advocates for deep, focused work without distractions. His strategies include:

- **Deep Work Blocks**: Newport schedules long, uninterrupted blocks of time for deep work, allowing him to concentrate fully on complex tasks.
- **Digital Minimalism**: He practices digital minimalism by limiting his use of social media and other digital distractions.
- **Environmental Design**: Newport designs his work environment to minimize distractions, ensuring it is quiet and free from interruptions.

Conclusion

Minimizing distractions and staying focused are crucial for entrepreneurs aiming to maximize productivity and achieve their business goals. By identifying common distractions, implementing effective strategies to maintain focus, and creating a productive work environment, you can

significantly enhance your concentration and efficiency.

Real-world examples from successful entrepreneurs like Elon Musk, Tim Ferriss, and Cal Newport demonstrate the power of these strategies in achieving high levels of productivity. By following their lead and applying these techniques, you can create a work environment that supports your goals and helps you stay focused on what truly matters.

Remember, the key to minimizing distractions and staying focused lies in understanding your unique challenges and proactively addressing them with tailored solutions. With practice and persistence, you can master the art of focus and drive your entrepreneurial success to new heights.

Chapter 7: Developing Productive Habits

Building a Routine

Building a routine is foundational for entrepreneurs aiming to boost productivity. A well-structured daily routine helps in organizing tasks, managing time efficiently, and maintaining a healthy work-life balance. Here's how to create and stick to a daily routine that promotes productivity:

Steps to Create a Productive Daily Routine

1. **Assess Your Current Schedule**

    - **Identify Time Wasters**: Analyze your current schedule to identify activities that consume time without adding value. Examples include excessive social media use, unnecessary meetings, and aimless web browsing.
    - **Track Your Time**: Use time-tracking tools like Toggl or RescueTime to monitor how you spend your day. This will provide insights into where your time goes and highlight areas for improvement.
    - **Link**: Toggl, RescueTime
2. **Set Clear Goals**

- **Long-Term Goals**: Define your long-term goals related to your business and personal life. These goals will guide your daily activities and ensure you stay focused on what matters.
- **Short-Term Goals**: Break down long-term goals into achievable short-term objectives. Set weekly and daily goals to maintain momentum and track progress.

3. **Prioritize Tasks**

    - **Eisenhower Matrix**: Use the Eisenhower Matrix to prioritize tasks based on urgency and importance. Focus on tasks that are both important and urgent.
    - **ABC Method**: Categorize tasks into A (high priority), B (medium priority), and C (low priority). Complete A tasks first, followed by B and C tasks.
    - **Link**: Eisenhower Matrix

4. **Time Blocking**

    - **Schedule Focused Work Periods**: Allocate specific blocks of time for focused work on high-priority tasks. Use tools like Google Calendar or Microsoft Outlook to set these time blocks.
    - **Include Breaks**: Schedule regular breaks to rest and recharge. The Pomodoro Technique, which involves working for 25 minutes

followed by a 5-minute break, is an effective method.
- **Link**: Google Calendar, Pomodoro Technique

5. **Morning and Evening Routines**

    - **Morning Routine**: Start your day with activities that set a positive tone, such as exercise, meditation, and planning your day. This can boost energy and focus.
    - **Evening Routine**: End your day with activities that help you unwind, such as reading, reflecting on your day, and preparing for the next day. This promotes better sleep and readiness for the next day.

6. **Eliminate Distractions**

    - **Digital Distractions**: Use website blockers like StayFocusd or apps like Freedom to limit access to distracting websites during work hours.
    - **Physical Environment**: Create a workspace that minimizes distractions. Keep it organized, well-lit, and equipped with necessary tools.

7. **Review and Adjust**

    - **Weekly Review**: Conduct a weekly review to assess your progress, identify challenges, and adjust your routine as needed. This ensures continuous improvement.

- **Flexibility**: Be flexible and open to adjusting your routine to accommodate unforeseen events or changing priorities.

Sticking to Your Routine

1. **Set Realistic Expectations**

   - **Achievable Tasks**: Ensure your daily tasks are realistic and achievable. Overloading your schedule can lead to burnout and frustration.
   - **Progress Over Perfection**: Focus on making consistent progress rather than achieving perfection. Small, steady improvements lead to long-term success.

2. **Accountability**

   - **Accountability Partner**: Share your goals and routine with an accountability partner who can provide support and encouragement.
   - **Public Commitment**: Announce your goals publicly to create a sense of accountability. This can be done through social media or within your professional network.

3. **Rewards and Incentives**

   - **Positive Reinforcement**: Reward yourself for sticking to your routine and achieving your goals. This can be as simple as taking a

break, enjoying a treat, or engaging in a favorite activity.
  - **Milestones**: Set milestones and celebrate reaching them. This keeps you motivated and provides a sense of accomplishment.

The Power of Consistency

Consistency is key to maintaining productive habits. It builds momentum, reinforces positive behaviors, and leads to sustainable success. Here's why consistency is important and how to cultivate it:

Importance of Consistency

1. **Habit Formation**

    - **21/90 Rule**: It takes about 21 days to form a habit and 90 days to make it a permanent lifestyle change. Consistent effort over time is essential for habit formation.
    - **Link**: 21/90 Rule
2. **Improved Efficiency**

    - **Routine Efficiency**: Consistency in following a routine reduces decision fatigue and enhances efficiency. When tasks become habitual, they require less mental energy and effort.

- **Mastery**: Repeated practice leads to mastery. Consistently performing tasks helps you become more skilled and proficient.

3. **Progress and Achievement**

    - **Incremental Progress**: Consistent effort leads to incremental progress, which accumulates over time and results in significant achievements.
    - **Goal Attainment**: Consistency ensures steady progress towards your goals. It helps in breaking down large goals into manageable steps and achieving them systematically.

4. **Reliability and Trust**

    - **Professional Reputation**: Consistency in delivering results builds reliability and trust with clients, partners, and team members.
    - **Self-Trust**: Consistent actions reinforce self-trust and confidence in your abilities to achieve your goals.

Cultivating Consistency

1. **Start Small**

    - **Small Steps**: Begin with small, manageable tasks that you can consistently accomplish. Gradually increase the complexity and scope of your tasks.

- **Micro-Habits**: Implement micro-habits, which are small actions that take minimal effort but contribute to larger goals. For example, spending 5 minutes each day planning your tasks.

2. **Use Triggers and Cues**

    - **Habit Stacking**: Attach new habits to existing ones. For example, if you already have a morning coffee routine, use that time to review your daily goals.
    - **Visual Cues**: Use visual cues like sticky notes, reminders, or habit-tracking apps to reinforce your habits and keep you on track.

3. **Maintain a Consistent Schedule**

    - **Regular Timing**: Perform tasks at the same time each day to create a sense of routine and predictability.
    - **Daily Rituals**: Establish daily rituals that signal the start and end of your workday, such as a specific morning routine or evening wind-down process.

4. **Monitor Your Progress**

    - **Habit Tracker**: Use a habit tracker to monitor your progress and stay accountable. This can be a simple checklist, a journal, or a digital app.
    - **Link**: Habit Tracker

5. **Adjust and Adapt**

    - **Flexibility**: Be flexible and willing to adjust your routine as needed. Life circumstances and priorities can change, and your routine should adapt accordingly.
    - **Resilience**: Develop resilience by not letting setbacks derail your progress. If you miss a day, get back on track the next day without feeling discouraged.

Avoiding Procrastination

Procrastination is a common challenge that can hinder productivity and delay goal attainment. Overcoming procrastination involves understanding its root causes and implementing strategies to address them.

Understanding Procrastination

1. **Psychological Factors**

    - **Fear of Failure**: Fear of making mistakes or not meeting expectations can lead to avoidance and procrastination.
    - **Perfectionism**: The desire to produce perfect results can cause delays in starting or completing tasks.

2. **Emotional Factors**

- **Lack of Motivation**: Low motivation or lack of interest in a task can result in procrastination.
- **Stress and Anxiety**: Stress or anxiety related to a task can lead to avoidance and procrastination.

3. **Cognitive Factors**

    - **Poor Time Management**: Inability to prioritize tasks or manage time effectively can contribute to procrastination.
    - **Overwhelm**: Feeling overwhelmed by the size or complexity of a task can cause procrastination.

Strategies to Overcome Procrastination

1. **Break Tasks into Smaller Steps**

    - **Micro-Tasks**: Break large tasks into smaller, manageable steps. This makes the task less daunting and easier to start.
    - **Progressive Steps**: Focus on completing one small step at a time. Each completed step builds momentum and confidence.

2. **Set Clear Deadlines**

    - **Self-Imposed Deadlines**: Set specific deadlines for each task and hold yourself accountable. Use calendar reminders or task management tools to stay on track.

- **Public Deadlines**: Announce your deadlines to others, creating external accountability and motivation to meet them.

3. **Use Time Management Techniques**

    - **Pomodoro Technique**: Use the Pomodoro Technique to break work into focused intervals with scheduled breaks. This can help maintain concentration and reduce procrastination.
    - **Time Blocking**: Allocate specific time blocks for different tasks, ensuring dedicated focus periods without interruptions.

4. **Create a Positive Work Environment**

    - **Minimize Distractions**: Eliminate or reduce distractions in your work environment. This includes digital distractions, noise, and clutter.
    - **Comfortable Workspace**:

5. **Comfortable Workspace**: Ensure your workspace is comfortable and conducive to productivity. This includes ergonomic furniture, proper lighting, and a clean, organized area.

5. **Address Underlying Issues**

    - **Identify Root Causes**: Reflect on why you are procrastinating. Is it due to fear of failure, perfectionism, or lack of interest?

Understanding the root cause can help you address it effectively.
- **Emotional Regulation**: Practice techniques like mindfulness, meditation, or deep breathing to manage stress and anxiety related to tasks.

6. **Incentivize Progress**

    - **Reward System**: Set up a reward system for completing tasks. Rewards can be small, such as taking a short break, enjoying a treat, or engaging in a favorite activity.
    - **Gamification**: Use gamification techniques to make tasks more engaging. This can include tracking progress, earning points, or competing with others.

7. **Seek Support and Accountability**

    - **Accountability Partners**: Work with an accountability partner who can provide support, encouragement, and hold you accountable for meeting your deadlines.
    - **Professional Help**: If procrastination is significantly impacting your productivity and well-being, consider seeking help from a coach or therapist who can provide strategies and support.

8. **Focus on the Benefits**

- **Visualize Success**: Visualize the positive outcomes of completing your tasks, such as achieving your goals, reducing stress, and feeling a sense of accomplishment.
- **Immediate Benefits**: Remind yourself of the immediate benefits of completing tasks, such as freeing up time for other activities and reducing the mental burden of unfinished work.

Real-World Examples and Case Studies

To illustrate the effectiveness of developing productive habits, let's explore some real-world examples and case studies of entrepreneurs who have successfully built routines, maintained consistency, and overcome procrastination:

Example 1: Jeff Bezos

Jeff Bezos, the founder of Amazon, is known for his disciplined approach to productivity and time management:

- **Morning Routine**: Bezos prioritizes getting enough sleep and starts his day with a healthy breakfast. He schedules high-priority meetings in the morning when he is most alert and focused.
- **Time Management**: He follows the "Two-Pizza Rule" for meetings, ensuring that no meeting is too large or unproductive.

- **Decision-Making**: Bezos practices "high-velocity" decision-making, focusing on making decisions quickly with 70% of the information rather than waiting for 100% certainty.

Example 2: Oprah Winfrey

Oprah Winfrey, a successful entrepreneur and media mogul, emphasizes the importance of routines and consistency in her life:

- **Daily Routine**: Winfrey starts her day with meditation and exercise, setting a positive tone for the rest of the day. She schedules time for reading and reflection, which helps her stay grounded and focused.
- **Consistency**: She maintains a consistent schedule for her work and personal life, balancing her commitments while ensuring she has time for self-care and relaxation.

Example 3: Tim Urban

Tim Urban, the creator of the popular blog "Wait But Why," has openly discussed his struggles with procrastination and how he overcame them:

- **Understanding Procrastination**: Urban explores the concept of the "Instant Gratification Monkey" and the "Panic Monster" to explain procrastination behaviors.

- **Structured Approach**: He uses structured time management techniques, such as breaking tasks into smaller steps and setting specific deadlines, to combat procrastination.
- **Public Accountability**: By sharing his journey and deadlines with his audience, Urban creates external accountability that motivates him to meet his goals.

Conclusion

Developing productive habits is essential for entrepreneurs aiming to maximize productivity and achieve their business goals. Building a routine, maintaining consistency, and overcoming procrastination are key components of this process.

By creating a structured daily routine, prioritizing tasks, and eliminating distractions, you can create an environment that fosters productivity and focus. Consistency reinforces positive behaviors and leads to sustainable success, while strategies to overcome procrastination ensure that you stay on track and make steady progress toward your goals.

Real-world examples from successful entrepreneurs like Jeff Bezos, Oprah Winfrey, and Tim Urban demonstrate the power of these strategies in achieving high levels of productivity. By following their lead and applying these techniques, you can develop habits that support your entrepreneurial journey and drive your success.

Remember, the journey to developing productive habits requires patience, persistence, and self-awareness. With commitment and practice, you can cultivate habits that enhance your productivity, reduce stress, and help you achieve your entrepreneurial aspirations.

Chapter 8: Work-Life Balance

In our modern, fast-paced world, finding a balance between work and personal life can often seem like an elusive goal. The demands of work, coupled with the ever-present distractions of technology and the pressures of daily life, can easily tip the scales, leaving us feeling overwhelmed and burnt out. However, maintaining a healthy work-life balance is not only essential for our well-being but also crucial for long-term success and happiness.

The Importance of Balance

Work-life balance is a critical component of long-term success for entrepreneurs. It involves creating a harmonious relationship between professional responsibilities and personal life, ensuring that neither aspect is neglected. Here's why maintaining this balance is crucial:

Benefits of Work-Life Balance

1. **Improved Health and Well-Being**

    - **Physical Health**: A balanced lifestyle allows for regular exercise, proper nutrition, and adequate sleep, which are essential for

physical health. Chronic stress from work can lead to health issues such as hypertension, cardiovascular diseases, and weakened immune function.
  - **Mental Health**: Balance reduces stress and anxiety, promoting better mental health. Chronic work stress is linked to mental health disorders like depression and burnout.
  - **Link**: Harvard Business Review on Work-Life Balance

2. **Enhanced Productivity and Creativity**

   - **Focused Work**: When personal life is in order, it's easier to concentrate on work tasks, leading to increased productivity and efficiency.
   - **Creative Thinking**: Time away from work allows the brain to relax and engage in creative thinking. Breaks and leisure activities can lead to innovative ideas and solutions.

3. **Stronger Relationships**

   - **Family and Friends**: Spending quality time with family and friends strengthens relationships, providing emotional support and a sense of belonging.
   - **Professional Relationships**: A well-balanced life fosters better communication and collaboration with

colleagues, leading to a more positive work environment.

4. **Sustainable Success**

   - **Preventing Burnout**: Consistent overwork can lead to burnout, characterized by emotional exhaustion, reduced performance, and disengagement. Balance prevents burnout and ensures sustainable career success.
   - **Long-Term Achievement**: Entrepreneurs with a balanced approach are more likely to maintain long-term motivation and drive, contributing to sustained success.

Real-World Examples

1. Sheryl Sandberg

   - Work-Life Integration: Sheryl Sandberg, COO of Facebook, advocates for work-life integration rather than a strict separation. She emphasizes setting priorities and making time for family while pursuing professional goals.
   - **Quote**: "The most important career decision you'll make is who your life partner is." - Sheryl Sandberg
   - **Link**: Sheryl Sandberg on Work-Life Balance

2. **Richard Branson**

- **Prioritizing Health and Family**: Richard Branson, founder of the Virgin Group, prioritizes health and family. He believes that maintaining a healthy lifestyle and spending time with loved ones are crucial for personal and professional success.
- **Quote**: "Take care of your employees, and they'll take care of your business." - Richard Branson
- **Link**: Richard Branson on Work-Life Balance

Setting Boundaries

Setting boundaries is essential to prevent work from encroaching on personal time. Clear boundaries help maintain a healthy work-life balance, ensuring that you can dedicate time to both professional and personal pursuits.

Steps to Set Effective Boundaries

1. Define Your Priorities

    - Personal and Professional Goals: Clearly define your personal and professional goals. Understanding what's important to you helps in setting boundaries that align with your priorities.
    - **Time Allocation**: Allocate specific times for work and personal activities. Ensure that both areas receive adequate attention.

2. **Create a Structured Schedule**

    - **Work Hours**: Set specific work hours and stick to them. Avoid working beyond these hours unless absolutely necessary.
    - **Breaks and Leisure**: Schedule regular breaks and leisure activities. Use these times to relax and recharge.
    - **Link**: Time Management Techniques
3. **Communicate Boundaries Clearly**

    - **With Colleagues and Clients**: Clearly communicate your working hours and availability to colleagues and clients. Set expectations about response times and availability outside of work hours.
    - **With Family and Friends**: Communicate your work schedule to family and friends, ensuring they understand when you are unavailable due to work commitments.
4. **Establish Physical Boundaries**

    - **Workspace**: Designate a specific workspace that is separate from your living areas. This physical separation helps in mentally distinguishing between work and personal time.
    - **Home Environment**: Create a home environment that supports relaxation and

personal activities. Avoid bringing work materials into personal spaces.

5. **Utilize Technology Wisely**

    - **Work Tools**: Use technology tools like calendars, project management software, and communication apps to organize and streamline work tasks.
    - **Do Not Disturb Mode**: Utilize "Do Not Disturb" modes on devices to minimize interruptions during personal time.
    - **Link**: Best Apps for Work-Life Balance

6. **Learn to Say No**

    - **Prioritize Requests**: Evaluate work requests and prioritize them based on importance and urgency. Learn to say no to tasks that do not align with your priorities or overload your schedule.
    - **Delegate Tasks**: Delegate tasks that can be handled by others. This frees up your time for high-priority activities and personal pursuits.

Overcoming Challenges in Setting Boundaries

1. **Guilt and Fear of Missing Out (FOMO)**

    - **Mindset Shift**: Shift your mindset to recognize that setting boundaries is essential for long-term success. Understand that saying

no to certain tasks allows you to say yes to more important ones.
    - **Positive Affirmations**: Use positive affirmations to reinforce the importance of maintaining boundaries and prioritizing self-care.
2. **Work Culture and Expectations**

    - **Advocate for Balance**: Advocate for a healthy work-life balance within your organization. Encourage policies that support flexible work arrangements and employee well-being.
    - **Lead by Example**: As an entrepreneur or leader, set an example by maintaining your own work-life balance. This sets a precedent for others to follow.

Self-Care and Stress Management

Self-care and stress management are critical for maintaining a healthy work-life balance. Entrepreneurs often face high levels of stress due to the demands of running a business. Implementing effective self-care and stress management strategies can significantly improve well-being and productivity.

Importance of Self-Care

1. **Physical Health**

- **Regular Exercise**: Incorporate regular exercise into your routine. Physical activity reduces stress, boosts energy levels, and improves overall health.
- **Balanced Diet**: Maintain a balanced diet rich in nutrients. Proper nutrition supports physical and mental well-being.

2. **Mental Health**

- **Mindfulness and Meditation**: Practice mindfulness and meditation to reduce stress and enhance focus. These practices promote mental clarity and emotional stability.
- **Adequate Sleep**: Ensure you get adequate sleep each night. Quality sleep is essential for cognitive function, mood regulation, and overall health.
- **Link**: Benefits of Meditation

3. **Emotional Well-Being**

- **Social Connections**: Maintain strong social connections with family, friends, and peers. Social support provides emotional stability and reduces feelings of isolation.
- **Hobbies and Interests**: Engage in hobbies and activities that bring you joy and relaxation. Pursuing interests outside of work helps in reducing stress and maintaining balance.

Strategies for Stress Management

1. **Identify Stressors**

    - **Work-Related Stressors**: Identify specific work-related stressors such as tight deadlines, high workload, or difficult clients. Understanding the sources of stress is the first step in addressing them.
    - **Personal Stressors**: Identify personal stressors that may impact your professional life. These can include family responsibilities, financial concerns, or health issues.

2. **Develop Coping Mechanisms**

    - **Relaxation Techniques**: Practice relaxation techniques such as deep breathing, progressive muscle relaxation, and guided imagery to manage stress.
    - **Time Management**: Use time management techniques to prioritize tasks and avoid last-minute rushes. Effective time management reduces stress and increases productivity.
    - **Link**: Stress Management Techniques

3. **Seek Professional Help**

    - **Therapy and Counseling**: Consider seeking therapy or counseling to address chronic stress or mental health issues. Professional support can provide valuable strategies and coping mechanisms.

- **Support Groups**: Join support groups or networks of entrepreneurs who face similar challenges. Sharing experiences and solutions can provide relief and insights.

4. **Implement Work-Life Integration**

    - **Flexible Work Arrangements**: Implement flexible work arrangements such as remote work, flexible hours, or compressed workweeks. Flexibility allows for better integration of work and personal life.
    - **Work-Life Harmony**: Strive for work-life harmony rather than a strict balance. Recognize that some periods may require more focus on work while others may allow for more personal time.
    - **Link**: Work-Life Integration Strategies

Real-World Examples and Case Studies

1. Arianna Huffington
    - Advocacy for Sleep: Arianna Huffington, founder of The Huffington Post and Thrive Global, advocates for the importance of sleep and self-care in achieving success. After experiencing burnout herself, she prioritized sleep and well-being, leading to increased productivity and creativity.
- **Quote**: "We think, mistakenly, that success is the result of the amount of time we put in at work,

instead of the quality of time we put in." - Arianna Huffington
- **Link**: Thrive Global
2. **Elon Musk**
    - **Balancing Work and Family**: Elon Musk, CEO of SpaceX and Tesla, emphasizes the importance of balancing work commitments with family time. Despite his demanding schedule, Musk makes time for his children and ensures he is present for important moments in their lives.
    - **Quote**: "If you're working 100 hours a week, you cannot do this sustainably for years. This is a recipe for mental and physical break down." - Elon Musk
    - **Link**: Elon Musk's Perspective on Work-Life Balance

Conclusion

Work-life balance is essential for entrepreneurs to maintain physical health, mental well-being, and sustainable success. Setting boundaries, prioritizing self-care, and managing stress are crucial components of achieving balance.

By defining priorities, creating structured schedules, and communicating boundaries effectively, entrepreneurs can prevent work from encroaching on personal time. Implementing self-care practices such as regular exercise, mindfulness, and adequate sleep helps in managing stress and promoting overall well-being.

Real-world examples from successful entrepreneurs like Sheryl Sandberg, Richard Branson, and Arianna Huffington demonstrate the importance of work-life balance in achieving long-term success. By prioritizing balance and integrating work and personal life effectively, entrepreneurs can lead fulfilling and sustainable careers while enjoying meaningful personal lives.

Remember, achieving work-life balance is an ongoing process that requires self-awareness, commitment, and adaptability. By prioritizing self-care and setting boundaries, entrepreneurs can create a lifestyle that supports both professional success and personal fulfillment.

○

Chapter 9: Continuous Improvement

In the fast-paced world of entrepreneurship, continuous improvement is not just a goal; it's a necessity. This chapter will delve into the critical aspects of evaluating and refining your time management practices, learning from mistakes, and staying adaptable to changes in your business landscape.

Evaluating Your Time Management Practices

Regular evaluation of your time management practices is essential to ensure that you are maximizing efficiency and productivity. Here are some methods for assessing and improving your time management techniques:

Time Audit

Performing a time audit involves tracking how you spend your time throughout the day. This allows you to identify time sinks, inefficiencies, and areas for improvement. Tools like Toggl or RescueTime can help automate this process by tracking your digital activities.

- **Toggl**: A time tracking tool that allows you to log your activities and analyze where your time is being spent.

- **RescueTime**: Automatically tracks time spent on websites and applications, providing insights into your digital habits.

Productivity Metrics

Measuring productivity metrics helps you gauge your effectiveness in completing tasks and achieving goals. Key metrics to consider include:

- **Task Completion Rate**: The percentage of tasks completed within a specified time frame.
- **Time Spent on High-Value Activities**: The proportion of time allocated to tasks that directly contribute to your business objectives.
- **Time to Task Completion**: The average time it takes to complete individual tasks.

Reflective Practice

Engaging in reflective practice involves regularly reflecting on your time management habits, identifying strengths and weaknesses, and setting goals for improvement. Journaling or using reflective prompts can facilitate this process.

- **Journaling**: Keep a daily or weekly journal where you record your thoughts, accomplishments, and areas for improvement related to time management.
- **Reflective Prompts**: Ask yourself questions such as, "What went well this week in terms of managing

my time?" and "What could I have done differently to be more productive?"

Learning from Mistakes

Mistakes are inevitable, but they also present valuable learning opportunities. Here's how you can effectively learn from past mistakes to refine your time management practices:

Root Cause Analysis

When a mistake occurs, take the time to analyze its root causes. This involves asking probing questions to uncover underlying issues and contributing factors. The "5 Whys" technique is a simple yet powerful method for digging deeper into the root causes of a mistake.

- **5 Whys Technique**: Ask "why" five times in succession to uncover the underlying causes of a mistake. This helps identify systemic issues rather than just surface-level symptoms.

Post-Mortem Analysis

Conducting a post-mortem analysis after a project or task is completed allows you to evaluate what went well, what didn't, and what lessons can be learned for the future. This process encourages honest reflection and fosters a culture of continuous improvement within your organization.

- **SWOT Analysis**: Assess the strengths, weaknesses, opportunities, and threats associated with a project or task. This comprehensive analysis helps identify areas for improvement and potential risks.

Growth Mindset

Embrace a growth mindset, which views mistakes as opportunities for learning and growth rather than failures. Cultivate resilience and optimism, and focus on what you can learn from each mistake to improve your future performance.

- **Carol Dweck's Work on Growth Mindset**: Explore the research of psychologist Carol Dweck, who coined the term "growth mindset" and has extensively studied the power of believing that abilities can be developed through dedication and hard work.

Adapting to Changes

In the dynamic world of entrepreneurship, adaptability is key to success. Here are strategies for staying flexible and adapting your time management practices as your business evolves:

Agile Methodology

Apply principles from agile methodology to your time management approach. Agile emphasizes iterative development, continuous feedback, and flexibility in response to changing requirements. Incorporate agile practices such as sprint planning, retrospectives, and daily stand-ups into your routine.

- **Scrum Framework**: Implement the scrum framework, a popular agile methodology used in software development, to organize and prioritize your tasks in short, focused intervals called sprints.

Experimentation and Iteration

Don't be afraid to experiment with new time management techniques and strategies. Adopt a mindset of continuous experimentation and iteration, where you test different approaches, gather feedback, and adjust your practices accordingly.

- **A/B Testing**: Apply A/B testing principles commonly used in marketing to your time management practices. Compare the effectiveness of different techniques by implementing them in parallel and measuring their outcomes.

Flexibility in Planning

While planning is essential, it's equally important to remain flexible in the face of unexpected changes and challenges. Build buffer time into your schedule to accommodate unforeseen events, and be prepared to adjust your plans as needed.

- **Contingency Planning**: Anticipate potential obstacles or disruptions that may arise and develop contingency plans to address them. This proactive approach minimizes the impact of unexpected events on your productivity.

Continuous Learning

Stay informed about emerging trends, tools, and best practices in time management and productivity. Dedicate time for continuous learning through reading books, attending workshops or webinars, and networking with peers in your industry.

- **Online Courses and Workshops**: Enroll in online courses or workshops focused on time management, productivity, and personal development. Platforms like Coursera, Udemy, and LinkedIn Learning offer a wide range of courses on these topics.

Conclusion

Continuous improvement is essential for entrepreneurs seeking to optimize their time management practices and achieve long-term success. By regularly evaluating your time management techniques, learning from mistakes, and staying adaptable to changes, you can enhance your productivity, effectiveness, and overall well-being.

Remember, improvement is a journey, not a destination. Embrace a growth mindset, remain open to feedback, and commit to ongoing learning and development. By continuously refining your approach to time management, you can position yourself for greater success and fulfillment in your entrepreneurial endeavors.

Conclusion

Congratulations on reaching the conclusion of "Time is Money: The Entrepreneur's Guide to Freeing Up Time." Throughout this book, we've explored a multitude of strategies and techniques aimed at helping entrepreneurs manage their time effectively, maximize productivity, and achieve a healthy work-life balance. As we wrap up, let's recap the key points discussed and offer some encouragement for your journey ahead.

Recap of Key Points

1. **Understanding the Value of Time**: We began by highlighting the importance of time management for entrepreneurs and its impact on business success. We explored how successful entrepreneurs prioritize and value their time, recognizing it as one of their most valuable assets.

2. **Setting Clear Goals and Priorities**: We discussed the significance of defining a clear vision and mission, setting SMART goals, and prioritizing tasks effectively to align with your objectives and maximize productivity.

3. **Planning and Scheduling**: We explored techniques for creating a daily schedule, implementing time blocking, and planning for the unexpected to optimize efficiency and adaptability

in your workflow.

4. **Leveraging Technology for Efficiency**: We recommended tools and apps for time management, automation of repetitive tasks, and effective communication and collaboration to streamline processes and enhance productivity.

5. **Delegating and Outsourcing**: We discussed criteria for delegating tasks, strategies for finding the right people, and best practices for managing outsourced tasks to leverage resources effectively and focus on high-value activities.

6. **Minimizing Distractions and Staying Focused**: We identified common distractions, shared techniques for maintaining focus, and provided tips for creating a productive work environment conducive to concentration and creativity.

7. **Developing Productive Habits**: We explored the importance of building a routine, maintaining consistency, and overcoming procrastination to cultivate habits that support long-term productivity and success.

8. **Work-Life Balance**: We emphasized the significance of maintaining a balance between work and personal life for overall well-being and sustainable success, offering strategies for setting

boundaries, prioritizing self-care, and managing stress.

9. **Continuous Improvement**: Finally, we discussed methods for evaluating time management practices, learning from mistakes, and staying adaptable to changes to continuously refine your approach and achieve greater efficiency and effectiveness.

Encouragement for the Journey

As you embark on implementing the strategies and techniques discussed in this book, remember that improvement is a continuous journey. Here are some words of encouragement to guide you along the way:

1. **Start Small, Iterate Often**: Don't feel overwhelmed by trying to implement all the strategies at once. Start with small changes, experiment, and iterate based on what works best for you and your business.

2. **Be Patient and Persistent**: Building effective time management habits takes time and consistency. Be patient with yourself and stay persistent in your efforts to improve. Celebrate small victories along the way and learn from setbacks.

3. **Stay Flexible and Adapt**: The entrepreneurial journey is full of twists and turns, and priorities may shift over time. Stay flexible in your approach to time management, and be willing to adapt your strategies as needed to align with changing circumstances.

4. **Seek Support and Accountability**: Don't hesitate to reach out for support from mentors, peers, or professional coaches who can provide guidance, accountability, and encouragement as you work towards your goals.

5. **Celebrate Progress, Not Perfection**: Remember that perfection is not attainable, but progress is. Celebrate the progress you make, no matter how small, and use setbacks as opportunities for learning and growth.

6. **Stay Inspired and Keep Learning**: Surround yourself with sources of inspiration and continue to invest in your personal and professional development. Stay curious, keep learning, and remain open to new ideas and opportunities.

Final Thoughts

Time is indeed money, but it is also much more than that. It's a finite resource that, when managed effectively, can unlock endless opportunities for growth, fulfillment, and success in both your business and personal life. By implementing the strategies outlined in this book and committing to continuous improvement, you have the power to take control of your time, unleash your potential, and create the life and business you desire.

Thank you for embarking on this journey with us. Here's to your continued success and fulfillment as an entrepreneur!

Recommended Reading:

- The Power of Habit by Charles Duhigg
- Deep Work by Cal Newport
- Atomic Habits by James Clear

Appendices

Recommended Tools and Resources

Tools for Time Management

1. **Calendar Apps**:

   - Google Calendar: A versatile calendar app for scheduling events, reminders, and tasks.
   - Microsoft Outlook: Offers calendar management, email integration, and collaboration features.

2. **Task Management Apps**:

   - Todoist: A task manager that helps you organize tasks, set priorities, and track progress.
   - Trello: A visual project management tool that uses boards, lists, and cards to organize tasks and collaborate with teams.

3. **Communication and Collaboration Tools**:

   - Slack: A messaging platform for team communication, file sharing, and collaboration.
   - Microsoft Teams: Combines chat, video meetings, file storage, and app integration in one platform.

4. **Time Tracking Software**:

    - Toggl: Tracks time spent on tasks and projects, generates reports, and analyzes productivity.
    - Harvest: Time tracking and invoicing software for tracking billable hours and managing projects.

Additional Recommendations

- **RescueTime**: Automatically tracks time spent on websites and applications, providing insights into digital habits and productivity.
- **Forest**: A mobile app that helps you stay focused and avoid distractions by planting virtual trees during work sessions.
- **Freedom**: Blocks distracting websites and apps across devices, allowing you to focus on important tasks.

Templates and Worksheets

1. **Daily Schedule Template**:

    - [Download Template](#)
    - Use this template to plan your daily activities and allocate time for tasks, meetings, and breaks.
2. **SMART Goals Worksheet**:

- Download Worksheet
- Use this worksheet to set specific, measurable, achievable, relevant, and time-bound goals for your business.

3. **Time Audit Tracker**:

    - Download Tracker
    - Track how you spend your time throughout the day to identify time sinks and areas for improvement.

4. **Reflection Journal Prompts**:

    - Use these prompts to reflect on your time management practices, identify strengths and weaknesses, and set goals for improvement.

Further Reading

Books

1. **"Deep Work: Rules for Focused Success in a Distracted World" by Cal Newport**: Explores the concept of deep work and offers strategies for maximizing focus and productivity in a world filled with distractions.

    - Amazon Link

2. **"Atomic Habits: An Easy & Proven Way to Build Good Habits & Break Bad Ones" by James Clear**: Provides practical advice on building habits

that support productivity and success.

- Amazon Link

Articles and Websites

1. **Harvard Business Review (HBR)**:

    - HBR offers a wealth of articles, case studies, and resources on time management, productivity, and entrepreneurship.
    - HBR Time Management Articles

2. **Entrepreneur.com** :

    - Entrepreneur.com publishes articles, guides, and expert advice on various aspects of entrepreneurship, including time management and productivity.
    - Entrepreneur Time Management Tips

3. **MindTools**:

    - MindTools provides practical tips, tools, and resources for personal and professional development, including time management techniques.
    - Time Management Tools and Techniques

Conclusion

The appendices of this book serve as a valuable resource for readers looking to implement the strategies discussed in the main chapters. From recommended tools and templates to additional reading materials, these appendices provide practical support for enhancing time management skills and fostering entrepreneurial success.

As you embark on your journey to free up time and maximize productivity, remember to leverage these tools and resources to support your efforts. Whether you're scheduling tasks, setting goals, or seeking further guidance, these resources are designed to help you achieve your goals and thrive as an entrepreneur.

Here's to your continued success and fulfillment in your entrepreneurial endeavors!

Recommended Reading:

- The Power of Habit by Charles Duhigg
- Getting Things Done by David Allen
- The 4-Hour Workweek by Timothy Ferriss

References

1. Duhigg, C. (2012). *The Power of Habit: Why We Do What We Do in Life and Business.* Random House. Link

2. Newport, C. (2016). *Deep Work: Rules for Focused Success in a Distracted World.* Grand Central Publishing. Link

3. Clear, J. (2018). *Atomic Habits: An Easy & Proven Way to Build Good Habits & Break Bad Ones.* Avery. Link

4. Sandberg, S. (2013). "Sheryl Sandberg on Work-Life Balance." *Inc.* Link

5. Branson, R. (2016). "Richard Branson's Guide to Work-Life Balance." *Virgin.* Link

6. Huffington, A. (2014). *Thrive: The Third Metric to Redefining Success and Creating a Life of Well-Being, Wisdom, and Wonder.* Harmony. Link

7. Musk, E. (2018). "Elon Musk Says This Should Be Your First Priority Every Day." *CNBC.* Link

8. Dweck, C. (2006). *Mindset: The New Psychology of Success.* Random House. Link

9. Mayo Clinic. "Meditation: A simple, fast way to reduce stress." Link

10. American Psychological Association (APA). "Stress Management." Link

11. Forbes Coaches Council. (2020). "10 Ways To Achieve Work-Life Integration Instead Of Balance." *Forbes*. Link

12. Toggl. Link

13. Todoist. Link

14. Trello. Link

15. Slack. Link

16. Microsoft Teams. Link

17. RescueTime. Link

18. Forest. Link

19. Freedom. Link

20. Harvard Business Review (HBR). Link

21. Entrepreneur.com. Link

22. MindTools. Link

23. Coursera. Link

24. Udemy. Link

25. LinkedIn Learning. Link

26. Amazon. Link

27. Getting Things Done. Link

28. The 4-Hour Workweek. Link

29. Allen, D. (2001). *Getting Things Done: The Art of Stress-Free Productivity.* Penguin Books. Link

30. Ferriss, T. (2009). *The 4-Hour Workweek: Escape 9-5, Live Anywhere, and Join the New Rich.* Harmony. Link

31. Mayo Clinic. "Time management: Tips to reduce stress and improve productivity." Link

32. MindTools. "Time Management." Link

33. Entrepreneur. "Time Management Tips for Entrepreneurs." Link

34. CNBC. "These time management hacks from self-made millionaires could help you reshape your day." Link

35. Thrive Global. "Arianna Huffington: On Work-Life Balance, Time Management, and the Importance of Well-Being." Link

36. Google Calendar. Link

37. Microsoft Outlook. Link

38. Todoist. Link

39. Trello. Link

40. Slack. Link

41. Microsoft Teams. Link

42. Toggl. Link

43. Harvest. Link

44. Forest. Link

45. Freedom. Link

46. Coursera. Link

47. Udemy. Link

48. LinkedIn Learning. Link

49. Amazon. Link

These references have been carefully selected to provide a comprehensive list of sources for readers who wish to further explore the topics discussed in this book. From books and articles to online courses and productivity tools, these resources offer valuable insights and practical guidance to support you on your journey toward mastering time management and entrepreneurship.

www.ingramcontent.com/pod-product-compliance
Lightning Source LLC
Chambersburg PA
CBHW082206220526
45470CB00010B/3064